194 Radio City
The Heart of Liverpool

Kathy Barham

Published by Lulu.com

First published in Great Britain in 2006 by
Lulu.com

Copyright © Kathy Barham 2006

The right of Kathy Barham to be identified as the author of this work has been asserted by her in accordance with the Copyright, Designs and Patens Act 1988

ISBN 978-1-4116-8814-8

All rights reserved. No part of this publication may be reproduced, transmitted or stored in a retieval system, in any form or by any means, without permission
in writing from Kathy Barham

Lyrics excerpt to "Give Me What I Cry For" by permission of Chris Rainbow & Vital Spark Music

Photographs by kind permission of the following:
Michael Green – Pages 5, 15, 16, 23, 24, 25. Radio City 96.7 – 11, 17, 32, 49, 55, 58, 81, 97, 98. Mark Jones – 27, 62, 64, 74. Bob Buckle – 68. Johnny Kennedy – 76. Dr Martin Van der Ven – 77. All other photographs submitted by the author

ACKNOWLEDGMENTS

I should firstly like to thank all the members of Radio City's staff, past and present, who so graciously allowed themselves to be interviewed by me over the last couple of years: Carolyn Brown, Bob Buckle, Joe Butler, Brian Cullen, Graham Dene, Kieran Devaney, Michael Green (not only for his memories, but also for allowing me access to his wonderful scrapbook of photos and transcripts), Howard Hughes, Johnny Jason, Paul Jordan, Chris Jones, Mark Jones, Rob Jones, Johnny Kennedy, Paul Leckie, Peter Levy, Dave Lincoln, Arthur Murphy, Gillian Reynolds MBE, Paul Rowley, Roy Saatchi, Simon Tate and Norman Thomas. To David Hamilton for talking at length about his memories of Dave Eastwood, and likewise to Richard Eastwood for chatting so candidly about his father's time at City and the later years. To all those at Essex Radio who provided such a wonderful picture of the man I lost touch with, and provided the basis from which this book eventually grew: Pete Sipple, Gavin McCoy, Peter Holmes, Brian Lee and Phil Hinton. To Eddie Boyes for memories of Dave in his pre-City days. To Sarah Smithard and Nick Parton for their own obsessive fan memories, likewise to Tony Hardaker for his side of the great ELO debate. Big thanks to Lesley Marshall for the wonderful collection of photographs of Radio City memories spanning the last 30 years. Dr Martin Van der Ven for the highly sought after, up-to-date photo of Johnny Jason. To Spencer Leigh for his advice, Mike 'Noddy' Knowler for the much appreciated copy of the 'Street to Street' LP featuring the '194 Radio City' song and his memories of its recording, and of course to Sharron Hendy, Nigel Bateman and Brian Jones for all their help in filling in the gaps with their encyclopaedic knowledge. And last but not least to Tom, Jonathan and Daniel for putting up with all this 194 nostalgia so patiently for so long.

... and Kathy would like to dedicate this to the following people:

To Tom, to Sharron "of course" and to the memory of Clive, Phil and Dave, all three of whom were tragically taken from us before their time; you are not forgotten and will always continue to inspire me.

This one's just for you....

Early DJ line up from 1978, l to r Chris Jones, Johnny Jason, Brian Cullen Norman Thomas and Dave Lincoln

Contents

Introduction	9
Chapter 1 A Journalist's Dream	11
Chapter 2 The Newsroom	23
Chapert 3 1976	32
Chapter 4 A Musical Education	37
Chapter 5 Rob Jones – A Crazy Love	43
Chapter 6 Downtown	48
Chapter 7 The Obsession Grows	53
Chapter 8 City Talk	55
Chapter 9 Home Thoughts from (not quite) Abroad	64
Chapter 10 Catching The Great Easton Express	66
Chapter 11 The Guitar Lessons	68
Chapter 12 Photographs and Memories	73
Chapter 13 Johnny Jason and the Great ELO Debate	77
Chapter 14 Jingle Jangle	81
Chapter 15 Dave Eastwood – A Musical Mentor	85
Chapter 16 The Radio City Retro Fest 2004	95
Postscript	99
Where are they now?	104

INTRODUCTION

In 2004, I made what was then a rare telephone call to my friend Sharron. Although we'd been friends for nearly 30 years, we seemed to have less in common than we once did. Marriage and children took precedence in my life, and Sharron, who had no real interest in either, did her own thing, as always. Many years ago it had been Liverpool's first independent radio station, Radio City, that had been our common bond and the reason we had become friends in the first place, and I wondered tentatively whether she would be interested in coming over on a Saturday night later in the month to celebrate Radio City's 30th birthday with me. I had decided to organise a 'Radio City Retro Fest'.

Radio City itself was holding a birthday concert in Liverpool during October, but we had no real interest in that. I had learned that Emap, the company who now owned the station, did not really believe in looking back, so there wouldn't be too much in the way of nostalgia accompanying their celebrations. What a missed opportunity. I felt that Sharron and I at least should acknowledge City in our own personal way along with a bottle or two of good wine. Sharron agreed straightaway and I advised her to bring anything she had that was City related, and any music that reminded her of that time.

I realise that the word 'Fest' will imply a rather large event, but this wasn't going to be anything like that, being attended by just Sharron and me. But it was to be a true 'Fest' in spirit. As we approached 42 years of age, this was to be a celebration of those happy, innocent teenage years from 1976 to the mid 1980s, when life lay tantalisingly ahead of us and Radio City seemed certain to play a large part in it. It certainly had been a vital part back then.

A vital part? Well, I believed this wasn't an exaggeration, and already the seeds were being sown in my mind of a book about a fan and her radio station, and I planned to put forward my idea to Sharron at the Retro Fest. There are lots of books out there about lads and their 'anorak' lifestyle. But few, if any, about girls and their obsessions. And although I had scoured the bookshops and the internet at length, I had been surprised to discover that not one book had ever been written about Radio City. No one appeared to remember just how big a part of people's lives it was in its early, golden years when it burst onto the scene as the country's ninth independent local radio station and grew in status every year, gathering awards with ease. I believed the time had come to put an end to this injustice. It was a story just begging to be told, and I wanted to be the one to tell it.

And why me? Well, from the age of 13 it would be fair to say that I had been obsessed with 194 Radio City, the music it played and DJs who played it - in fact anyone or anything connected with the station. Like most obsessions, it had faded eventually, but in this case, I found it was remarkably easy to recapture the original feeling of euphoria the station had given me. Just hearing the old adverts and jingles could set me off. And I soon began to wonder about the people I remembered as being part of my listening years - the DJs, the newsreaders and those behind the scenes. What were they all doing now? Did they remember the same things as Sharron and me? Did they even care what happened 30 years ago? Was it all as blissfully happy inside the studios as it sounded to us as we listened in awe from our bedrooms?

So you will see that this book is not simply a straightforward history of the station. Although, alongside my own reminiscences I do set out to try to uncover what and who made the station so great, it is not simply a list of facts, events and names. May I apologise here if I have omitted what you feel is the most important aspect of the station, but this is my personal picture of my radio station. If you listened back then, I know you will have your own memories, so compare, contrast and hopefully rediscover your own.

A JOURNALIST'S DREAM

Terry Smith in the brand new studios at Stanley Street prior to launch, October 1974

When the idea first came to me to write a book about what I believe was for a time the country's finest radio station, I was expecting to discover exactly what made 194 Radio City so special, particularly in the 1970s and early 1980s. Maybe I would find something within the balance of its shows, its uniquely local feel, the wide coverage of all types of music. Instead I quickly found that Radio City was on the face of it no different from any other independent local radio station around at that time. It was bound by the same rules and restrictions, which included just nine hours of popular music allowed to be played in any one day at the time. It had to cover all genres of music as well as providing local interest and specialist programmes, and having to have its own news team. So that was nothing innovative, rather something that had been forced upon it. But this hadn't been such a massive success in other parts of the country, so what was different in Liverpool? Why did the awards so often come flooding in Radio City's direction? The people who started it all were

194 Radio City

Terry Smith, David Maker and Gillian Reynolds. They certainly had a firm picture of exactly what it was that the Liverpool listener wanted, and they intended from the outset to create not just a local station, but a great local station. Consequently, in the early days there were lots of changes; if something didn't work straightaway then it would be dropped, unceremoniously and quietly. Move on, try something else. And there were unfortunate casualties which we shall discover later. In that sense then, the station was free to experiment, much more than would be possible nowadays. But the straightjacket was there nonetheless. How they managed to make it all gel together in such a natural-sounding way was pure genius. But after all this time, I have to admit that I'm still none the wiser about exactly what 'it' was.

Independent broadcasting was introduced to Britain via the Independent Broadcasting Act and was one year old on 8th October 1974. On the 21st of that same month, Radio City, Liverpool's newest station was born. It is hard to believe now, but at the time it was only the ninth independent station in the country, and was the only one outside London to broadcast 24 hours a day. Up until this auspicious date, radio for the masses was predictable, conservative and safe. The BBC had a stranglehold on the country's listening needs. When pirate radio stations fought to play what people really wanted to hear, they were unceremoniously stopped and those involved treated as nothing less than hardened criminals. Many of the pirate DJs found themselves in court charged with 'abetting the operation of an illegal radio vessel'. They were often heavily fined.* It was clear that the establishment were afraid of any media that was not directly under their control; so much for democracy. And, although legal, even trying to listen to Radio Luxembourg in the 1970s remained notoriously frustrating due to temperamental signals.

Radio 1 was brought in to tap into the market for young listeners and it actually employed a great many of the ex-pirate DJs. But it wasn't innovative in its structure.

For all legitimate stations, 'Needletime' restrictions existed. For the uninitiated, 'Needletime' was the permitted quota of commercial, or 'pop' records that a station was allowed to play. Local BBC radio stations sprang up, but really as it was still the BBC, there wasn't much to get excited about. Having said that, BBC Radio Merseyside, it must be acknowledged had a

* *Future Radio City star, Johnny Jason was one such 'criminal' but he decided not to accept the charge and along with his lawyer, went on to fight the courts, eventually escaping on what was termed a 'technicality' at the time.*

The Heart of Liverpool

huge audience. It had been around since 1967 and any new station would have a difficult job trying to break into its proven territory.

The Independent Broadcasting Authority had chosen Radio City from four applicant groups and out of these, a company called 'Sound of Merseyside' was the only local company. The senior staff of this company were led by Merseyside journalist Terry Smith, who had previously operated the Mercury Press News Agency in Liverpool. He took on the role of Managing Director. Working alongside him as News Editor was another journalist, David Maker, and Programme Controller was Oxford graduate Gillian Reynolds, who had previously worked as a TV researcher and radio critic of The Guardian newspaper. Gillian explains how she became involved. "I knew Terry because his news agency did work for ABC TV, for whom I did a lot of work in the 1960s. I knew David through BBC Radio Merseyside. Terry approached me about the Radio City franchise bid after an article I wrote for the magazine of the Merseyside Arts Association, about what a local commercial radio station could add. I agreed to become part of the team and was a lead player in the written and in person submissions to the IBA, in 1972. I joined the staff formally on 1 April 1973."

Others who were there right at the beginning were Chairman Ken Medlock, Chief Engineer Peter Duncan, Sales Manager James Dandy, Company Secretary Norman Noonan and Marketing Manager Peter Hulm.

It had been Terry's dream for a little under five years to set up a local radio station in Liverpool. At the time, he had still been working as a journalist and began to look around for like-minded people. This search took four and a half years, and only then could they apply for the contract.

The basic idea behind the company's bid was that it was to be run by Merseysiders for Merseysiders. In fact, almost without exception, everyone involved was from the local area, and those few that weren't born there had lived or worked there so long, they could now be called honorary Merseysiders. Shareholders included comedian Ken Dodd and scriptwriter Carla Lane, who were hugely respected in the 1970s.

Terry managed to get their 'manifesto' for the company in for the bidding exactly one week early. This made them look extremely confident, although Terry, a staunch supporter of Liverpool Football Club and who now sits on the board, later admitted it was only because he wanted to be available the next week to watch his team play in the UEFA cup in Belgrade.

The introduction to the manifesto, which was printed in part in the Liverpool Echo on 11th October 1974, contained some strong claims. "When the new Liverpool independent station starts to broadcast it will either belong to the local people and become part of their lives very quickly, or it will be rejected. If it truly identifies itself with the locality and understands its many moods and backgrounds, it will be immediately accepted, and its occasional failure cheerfully forgiven.

"For the first time in very many years, Merseysiders have an opportunity to do it all for themselves."

Terry was also adamant that the station should run for the full 24 hours. "In our application for the Merseyside contract we indicated that we would be proposing 24-hour broadcasting and it has always been our intention to do that" he explained. "It has always been our aim to become the North West's major source of news and information, and only 24-hour broadcasting can achieve that."*

'Sound of Merseyside' found itself on the final shortlist of two and Terry prepared to travel to the interview, but this was the era of the power crisis, which included petrol rationing. Terry, the story goes, realised that funeral cars were exempt from rationing and hired two of them, despite everyone else's misgivings that it might be tempting providence. However, Terry pointed out that when you travel in a funeral car you are going to someone else's funeral and not your own.

The day following the interview, Terry was given the good news that they had won the contract at 7.25 am, but was told he was unable to share it with everyone else for a further eight hours when it would then be official. Only then could the celebrations and, of course, the really hard work begin.

The building itself which would house Radio City's studios and offices, nos 8-10 Stanley Street, was previously a commercial building and was set within the warehouse district of Liverpool, just around the corner from rival station, BBC Radio Merseyside. It had been completely transformed inside a period of just five months into a building which housed three modern radio studios with the most high-tech equipment of the day. In fact they were rated as being one of the most modern in Europe. Peter Hulm, the station's marketing manager explained in the Liverpool Echo on 11th October 1974. "They took the building apart, took the inside out literally. Just imagine the structural alterations that had to be made to find the space for three stereo studios broadcasting 24 hours a day. The equipment was so intricate and delicate to move.

"Altogether a staff of 60 will man the station, including 18 journalists, about 12 announcers and a sales team of five. There is also a London sales

* *Script Magazine 14.11.74 "Liverpool On The Air"*

The Heart of Liverpool

team to canvass national advertising. We've got no "Off" switch. When we press the button we start broadcasting and we don't stop."

The Radio City transmitters covered one of the most densely populated areas in the United Kingdom at the time with a population of well over two million. Staff were confident that they would become the most successful commercial station in the country because at the time, reception of BBC Radio 1 was very poor in the area. Radio Caroline remained popular but BBC Radio Merseyside would be the main competition.

8-10 Stanley Street – work in progress 1974

All very hi-tech and exciting. But when you speak to people about their memories of the Stanley Street studios now, hi-tech is not the immediate thing that comes to mind.

Gillian Reynolds recalls "My most vivid memory of Stanley Street is our Chairman, Ken Medlock, lending a hand with the rest of us by brushing the floors the day before we went on air. Before that, when none of us had any furniture, David Maker and I made a desk out of cardboard packing cases - it looked really convincing! And before that, when we very first began and before we moved into Stanley Street, Terry, David Maker, Peter Duncan and

I worked out of Terry's offices in Manchester Street and what I remember very vividly are the sacks and sacks of tapes from would-be DJs that were waiting for me on the very first day."

Gillian Reynolds, Programme Controller, 1974

Michael Green of the news team also recalls the makeshift furniture and "sitting on cardboard boxes in an empty Stanley Street office while the building work continued and new members of staff arrived."

One of the first DJs to secure a job on Radio City was Graham Dene, now on Magic FM in London. "I think I arrived from London about 2-3 weeks prior to launch and Gillian Reynolds had handed me the job of Music Director, which was met with deep resentment by a couple of the presenters, especially as I was far more Top 40 orientated than they were. Another of my tasks was to discover a local air talent. Nothing stood out until I came to the final tape on the final search day. I took it to Gillian and said "this is so bad, its good." She agreed and hired Rob Jones. This saved Rob from a life of accountancy!"

The very first record to be played on air on 21st October 1974 was 'You Are The Sunshine Of My Life' by Stevie Wonder, and the first DJ to broadcast on that day was Arthur Murphy. Arthur had a style all of his

The Heart of Liverpool

own, as engineer and DJ Chris Jones recalls "Arthur became something of a legend. Some schools had Arthur Murphy appreciation societies. There are so many 'Arthur' stories." The show Arthur presented from 6am on 21st October 1974 was 'The Breakfast Show'. Dublin-born Arthur was no stranger to the North West of England as he had been a presenter on BBC Look North in the 1960s which, at that time, transmitted to Cheshire, Lancashire and Yorkshire. "The reason I joined City was that I wanted to gain experience of using a self-operational desk and the rest of the studio

Mike McCartney with DJ Graham Dene, 1974

equipment. RTE Radio (in Eire) being a semi-State organisation, was, like the BBC, heavily unionised. There were guys who operated the record turntables, sound engineers who controlled the microphones, a producer etc. At City, one had to do all these jobs. At RTE, if you had tried to do any of the above jobs, there would have been a strike."

Arthur remembers the station's beginnings very well. "At the beginning there was a great atmosphere at City. Everyone mucked in to get the station on air for the set date. So far as I know we all arrived 3 weeks before the opening. I remember it was well past midnight the day before opening and even though I would have to be up at 5 am the same day, I, with Peter Duncan and others, were helping to to lay the carpet in the reception area."

Norman Thomas had applied for a job at the station after returning to the UK from Canada where he had worked on the radio for a company called CFJR in Brockville, Ontario. He had received on-air experience, and Norman explained how this had been following on from the era of The Beatles, when it had been easy to get a job on a station abroad if you had anything that sounded remotely like a Liverpool accent. Once back in the UK, he heard about the new station starting up in Liverpool, but although he applied for the job, he heard nothing. Eventually he telephoned Gillian Reynolds to say that, although he accepted he hadn't got the job, could she please keep his name in case any other jobs came up in future and she told him that she was so glad he had phoned because the station had lost his number and they very much wanted him to work at Radio City. Norman of course accepted, and started straightaway. He remained at the station for many years, becoming one of the most well-known and best-loved DJs.

One of Norman's most vivid memories is how, on the very first day, everyone arrived to find the studios covered with flowers. It looked fabulous and staff were informed by chairman, Ken Medlock, that they had been sent by famous well-wishers such as Paul McCartney and Cilla Black. This certainly boosted morale, however, the truth was revealed several months later by Ken who admitted that they had actually been provided by a friend who worked in a local funeral parlour.

In 1974, 20 year old Dave Lincoln was a time-served electrician from Sheffield when he was accepted from amongst the sackfuls of hopefuls to start his first professional radio job on Radio City. "I had worked on hospital radio" says Dave "and had served my five year apprenticeship with Thorn Electrics, and having passed my exams was obviously set to do well, so you can imagine how my parents reacted when I announced that I wanted to give up all this security for a job as a DJ." But Dave had been unhappy that his life was not going the way he'd wanted it to, and saw this job at a brand new radio station as a great opportunity which, if he let it go, may never be repeated. There was only one choice as far as he was concerned, and that was radio. Like everyone else who was there at the outset, he remembers the panic before opening. "The day before opening, the building was still not ready, although the studios were. It was a big thing. The press were inside the building waiting to see the launch of a new station. I was actually taken on to cover the middle of the night show which started off as the training ground for new presenters. However Les Ross, who was supposed to cover the 2 pm to 6 pm show decided at the last

The Heart of Liverpool

minute to stay in Birmingham, so I was given that show." A lucky break. Dave went on to become one of the most popular and successful DJs.

The launch programme was handled by Liverpool-based agency, Leighton Advertising. They spent around £75,000 getting the station noticed. In the local papers, on bus stops and even on TV, potential listeners had been given flashes of what this new station would be. Kevin Keegan, Cilla Black, Gerry Marsden and Dave Clements adorned posters claiming that Radio City was their station. "If you live on Merseyside" ran the ads "then Radio City is for you. Our very own Radio Station. All the programmes you want, whatever you want, from local sport to local music and local people. The Breakfast show, City Extra, Hotline, Happy is the Bride, The War Years and music to please all-brows. First on the dial on 194 metres Medium Wave."*

There was also a cut-out-and-keep guide to the programmes, which showed the variety on offer right from the start. Shows such as 'Venue', an outside broadcast show from all types and locations within the region. This was presented by Norman Thomas who has fond memories of this time. "(Venue) went out three times a week" he recalls. "We travelled around in a big Winnebago wagon kitted out to do outside broadcasts with huge microphones on leads. It was a very clever idea because what would happen was that we'd go to, say, a factory and chat to the workers there, and of course they'd all tune in the next day to hear themselves and hopefully would enjoy the show for itself and stay with us, which they usually did. That show was great for me. I learned so much about broadcasting, and how to ad-lib."

There was also 'Sounds Local', news of local theatre, music, sport, books religion and the arts. 'Hotline', a phone-in with local experts, 'Downtown', which was a completely different show at the outset from what it eventually became, containing back then studio guests, reviews of plays, concerts and social events, sports coverage and match reports 'Cash and Grab', a weekly competition programme with prizes. 'Pub Call', a weekly visit to a local pub with music, quizzes, jokes and "at-the-bar chat". 'Reporting 74' a documentary programme based on Merseyside looking at important issues of the day, locally and nationally. 'Concert Hall' for classical music lovers. 'Starspin' hosted by Kevin Keegan and Dave Clements - Liverpool and Everton were always equally represented on City - with music, interviews, opinions and lots of chat, and 'Plod's Patrol', John Gorman's half hourly comedy show about a fictional policeman.

* *advertising campaign run in the Liverpool Echo prior to launch, 11th October 1974*

194 Radio City

There was even 'The 78 Show', which played authentic, scratchy oldies. Something for everyone then. *

As for the music format, initially it lay somewhere between middle-of-the-road and pop. The format throughout the day was to sound very relaxed and free. Only one hour of phone-in programmes was to be broadcast on the station every day. There were plans for live broadcasts of concerts featuring every type of music and the hourly lunchtime show every day was an outside broadcast.

So what were my memories of this great and historic time? Well, I have none, I'm ashamed to say. When the station launched, I was 11 years old and still very much into Mike Batt and the Wombles - one thing Radio City surprisingly didn't cover in great detail!

I had been brought up, thanks to my parents, on a varied musical diet which included 60s pop, a wide classical base, and the Big Bands, so was already a bit of a music-head. Strangely, although I was vaguely aware of a new radio station being launched on Merseyside I had no real sense of its importance. I could never have guessed what a huge effect it would have on my approaching adolescence. If I had, I might have taped some of those early shows. We did have a tape recorder; one of those rectangular mono ones with huge buttons on the bottom and a microphone you plugged in and switched on and then held in front of the radio or TV set. It was, I recall, a very clumsy affair.

I do have recordings of 'Top of The Pops' from that time, and even myself participating in a show on BBC Radio Merseyside where my school read poetry we had written about the sea. (The opposition, how could I?) About all I can definitely remember about City's launch is a very brief few minutes, sometime within the first week - it could have been the first day, I like to think it was - when my mother tuned in to see what all the fuss was about. Not much obviously, as I wasn't to hear it again at home for a couple of years. Unfortunately, I have no recollection of who the DJ was, what music was being played, or even of registering any of the fabulous 70s jingles. All this wonder was to come much later for me.

In the meantime, Radio City carried on without me. Someone who was lucky enough to be listening to Radio City from day one was future presenter, Paul Leckie. At the time he was only 14 years old, but his mum, Eileen, had secured a secretarial post at the station and Paul was able to meet his favourite DJs as he regularly visited the studios. "As Mum

* *Extracts from 'This Is What 194 Radio City Will Sound Like' from the Liverpool Echo 18th October 1974.*

The Heart of Liverpool

worked at City, I heard all the usual gossip and stories of the presenters" remembers Paul. "Arthur Murphy was one of my favourites. I loved his style and humour and, at that time, he was the only presenter with professional experience. I especially remember going to see Linda Lewis and Labi Siffre in concert at the Empire Theatre; a truly magical evening. I was introduced to Arthur by my mum. He had to leave the concert early to go on air at 10 pm but he asked us both to pop in. Naturally, I was thrilled.

"When the show was over, Mum and I both walked up to the Stanley Street Studios and I seem to remember it was Bert, the Commissionaire - he wore a uniform with a commissionaire's sash- who opened the door. He just told us to go straight through to the studio.

"In those days, Studio 1 was the large studio at the back. From reception you could see straight through central control, over the corridor and could clearly see the DJ on air - all very exciting. I especially remember the new, fresh smell of the carpets as I went through the corridor and of pushing the heavy studio door to meet Arthur. It seemed quite strange meeting the DJ I had listened to and admired for so long. Arthur shook hands and allowed me to sit directly behind him and showed me how the desk worked. I remember him with his headphones on, tapping his feet as he talked over the music and even playing his own songs 'Please Remember Me' and 'Shuffling Clay', which were released on vinyl.

"The studio was magical and had wall to wall settees all around and green and yellow guest microphones, which I vividly remember.

"Going back to school the next day, I knew that I too wanted to be a DJ at my local station." But that, of course, wouldn't be for some time yet.

Different memories remain for Graham Dene, who had secured his first proper radio station job after working at the industrial radio station UBN. Based at the United Biscuits factory in Osterley, West London, it is now the home of Tesco and Sky TV. UBN broadcast to various factories around the country via Post Office landlines and Graham hosted the 10 am to 2 pm show between the years 1970 and 1974.

On his first day in Liverpool, he had driven up from London in an old Lotus convertible. "With nowhere to live and everything I owned in the vehicle I left the soft-top car on some nearby wasteland" Graham recalls. "Within an hour the police were on the phone to say it had been broken into. Fortunately, they grabbed the culprit as he was doing it and I was saved. The site of the early studios didn't really instil a feeling of showbiz grandeur. Stanley Street wasn't exactly an attraction, apart from the wine bar across the road. Inside though, no problem. It was well equipped and felt like a buzzy radio station should."

194 Radio City

Radio City managed to do everything it seemingly set out to do, and things which perhaps it would have preferred remained forgotten. Such as the time Arthur Murphy made a somewhat rude apology on air. Like most radio stations, Radio City had a list of records which DJs weren't allowed to play, and this included some records containing swear words. One day, Arthur unknowingly played one of these and one of the other members of staff in the studio turned to him in disbelief and said "you stupid twat, Arthur". When the record finished, Arthur said to the listeners live on air "I've just been called a stupid twat!" During the next record, someone had a quiet word with him and after that record had finished, to everyone's horror, Arthur said to his audience "I'd just like to apologise to you listeners out there for saying 'stupid twat'. I didn't realise it was a swear word."

Gillian Reynolds remembers a few disasters early on too. "There was one night when the regular phone-in guy didn't turn up and I stood in for him, with Bill Bingham working the panel. All was going well, except we didn't have the 'delay' mechanism on, and I was chatting away to the callers when someone came on and said - without the delay - "Yer a load of fuckin' wankers" and I managed to say "And now on Line 6..." There was also the time when Michael Green (who used to play the gardening expert, 'Sefton Park', on 'The 78 Show', as well as being a newsroom star) went into the newsbooth to do a bulletin and found there was no microphone; someone had nicked it for a studio session. And there was the time when Elton John came and his brown Rolls Royce got a parking ticket..."

THE NEWSROOM

The Newsroom, 1974

The DJs weren't the only people excited at the prospect of setting up a new station. There was a brand new newsroom with David Maker at the helm. David Maker had worked in journalism on Merseyside for the vast majority of his professional life, spending time both on newspapers and in radio. Having had the opportunity to see the news as reported in both these formats, he was convinced that radio was the fastest news medium around. He brought this belief with him to Radio City and he explained in the Liverpool Echo prior to the launch that "what in fact we've done is to design a station which establishes that philosophy. Merseyside is a unique area with unique talents, problems, doubts and enthusiasms, and the radio station to reflect all this must speak with an individual voice."

So Arthur Murphy goes down in history as being the first DJ to broadcast on City, but the first words actually heard were from the Radio City news team. And Michael Green was the very first newsreader, although it perhaps wasn't as auspicious an occasion as it should have been. He can now admit that the first broadcast was the only time the news did not go out live. David Maker allegedly could not overcome his nervousness the day before launch, and insisted the very first news slot be pre-recorded in case of any mistakes.

David Maker told the potential new listeners in the Liverpool Echo in September 1974 why the news team was so important. "No other form of mass communication can take away from radio its rightful claim to be the first with the news. Radio news is instant - its as fast as a man can speak. The first words on the great news events of our time - from the conquest of Everest to the tragedy of Aberfan - were brought to the world by radio.

David Maker, News Editor, 1974

"We at Radio City are busy capitalising on the natural advantage radio presents to the journalist. We have a news staff of 16. News broadcasters, duty editors, reporters and specialists: local government editor, industrial correspondent and sports editor."

There were also fully equipped news cars in which were fitted both VHF and UHF circuits. The first for newsroom to car communication, and the second for broadcasting. It was boasted that the news staff had small radio

The Heart of Liverpool

microphones which were the size of a carton of cigarettes, with the ability to broadcast direct to the studios from any situation.

"Our determination to be where the action is will be the hallmark of Radio City News." concluded the piece. "And if the day should come when the sky falls in on Merseyside, I can assure you that you will hear about it first on Radio City News."

Memories of the newsroom are still clear after all these years. Carolyn Brown, now resident on BBC Radio 4, recalls. "The newsroom was on the first floor (with) one big desk that we all sat round with a variety of clunky manual typewriters. At one end, a big vertically wall-mounted reel-to-reel

Mike Green and Kieran Devaney setting off from Liverpool in 1979 on the Liverpool – Beaujolais Run. Note the 194 Radio City Sunvisors.

tape machine that looked quite hi-tech in those days, which clicked into life whenever IRN (Independent Radio News) in London sent us news 'cuts' These were recorded on 'carts' - tape cartridges like the old eight-tracks we had in cars at the time. Next to that was a sort of kitchen counter where we assembled the carts and their associated intros and scripts into actual bulletins. Next to that were two reel-to-reel machines where we could edit taped interviews we'd brought back to the office."

And Howard Hughes, who as a novice newsreader learned his craft live on air and who has now become a highly successful presenter in his own right, recalls how the news could sometimes be shared between stations. "We used to trade news reports with Piccadilly in Manchester - reports from places we both covered, like Warrington and Wigan. These days everything is on studio quality ISDN-links. Then even our contributions to the IRN network were by telephone.

"At the end of a solo, 10 hour overnight news shift, the incoming breakfast team - often including the News Editor - would pick through what you had written overnight. It was like taking an exam and just as frightening. And you'd failed if BBC Radio Merseyside had a story you hadn't found!"

The late Ron Davies, who was famous of course for covering the 'Traffic and Travel' reports and for his friendly banter with the presenters, managed to get a job with Radio City in quite an unorthodox way. Apparently he used to listen in to the police band on the radio and he would then phone Radio City and tip the newsreaders as to where the news was happening so they could dash round and be first at the scene. The police could never work out how they got there so quickly.* When a job then came up for a 'Traffic and Travel' reporter, the news team suggested it was given to Ron, and he became a long-standing favourite voice on the station. Unfortunately, Ron passed away in 2003, but is still remembered by a great many listeners from over the years.

And then, of course there was Roy Saatchi. There are some wonderful stories about his time at Radio City. For instance how once, whilst making an outside broadcast from the entrance of the Birkenhead Tunnel he was accosted by the tunnel police live on air half way through a traffic bulletin, and told to move on as he wasn't allowed to stop there. There is also the time when he panicked, feeling sure that he'd seen a bomb being thrown through an open window in the Stanley Street building. The studios were immediately evacuated and the whole of Stanley Street ended up being closed off as it was investigated, however it turned out to be nothing

---

* *This is remarkably similar to the case of the American photographer, Arthur Fellig (1899 - 1968). Nicknamed 'Weegee' a phonetic spelling of Ouija, this name came about due to his arrival at the scene only minutes after crimes, fires or other emergencies were reported. He was able to do this due to the fact that he listened in to police-band short wave radio in his car.*

The Heart of Liverpool

more than a packet of coffee that someone had left on a window sill. Being a stuffy room, the window was open and a gust of wind had blown the packet back into the room. A somewhat serious man, he was also clearly not averse to lightening up a little when no one was looking, such as the time when he used the opening words to a famous Simon and Garfunkel song to cover the weather insert at the start of the through the night news bulletins: "A winters day in a deep and dark December, and this is Roy Saatchi with Radio City news".

Recently he received an honorary professorship award for services to journalism from the Liverpool John Moores University, appropriately enough, alongside one Terry Smith who was being honoured for his work with Radio City.

Mark Jones, Phil Easton, Sue Toshack (wife of footballer, John), Chris Jones, Bill Dingham and Roy Saatchi at a Wellie Throwing Competition, 1979, Marine FC's Ground (The winner was Mark Jones, apparently!)

He crammed a lot into his otherwise short time in Liverpool, including meeting and marrying his wife, but I feel I must make a confession to Roy.

194 Radio City

I was the 14 year old girl who in 1977 made a strange phone call to the Saatchi household and, I think, rather scared him.

My schoolfriend Debbie and I were undertaking a school project which concerned people and their jobs. I can't recall what the outcome of it all was going to be, but one of the parts involved interviewing several people about their jobs - all very boring, however I decided we could liven it up significantly by including a famous name or two from 194. When a scoop that would be.

Of course, it would have been far too easy to contact Radio City and explain my aim and very possibly be allowed to speak to one of the members of staff - although, knowing my luck, it would probably have been Bert, the doorman! No, I decided quite simply to scour the phone book for likely names and very soon I located a Mr R Saatchi who was then at an address in Birkenhead.

Debbie and I crammed ourselves, giggling, into a phone box in Moreton on the very next Saturday afternoon and I dialled the number, feeling absolutely terrified.

"Hello?" The phone was answered a lot quicker than I expected and I was taken by surprise.

"Er... Can I speak to Roy Saatchi please?"

"Speaking". Oh God!

I explained about my school project. There was a pause.

"How did you get my number?" He sounded pretty scared, and this was in the days before stalkers were commonplace, so God only knows what he thought was going on.

"From the phone book."

"Oh". He still sounded worried - and why shouldn't he? After all, it was now clear I would have access to his address as well. I pictured him looking around, checking outside the window - where was I phoning from? Was I watching his house?

There was an ominous silence but rather than panicking, I decided I just had to get on with the intended interview and, to be fair, after this painful start, he was actually very helpful, answering all my inane questions. I can't remember most of them now, however I do remember the last one which concerned the highlight of his City years. I remember he said it was being asked to cover the death of Elvis Presley.

I thanked him and he actually asked me if his answers had been OK. I probably gushed. After all, I was so excited. No one else in the class would have a Radio City person on their project, I was sure.

The Heart of Liverpool

I'd like to apologise to Roy for having made him so undeservedly nervous, and also for having the naive audacity to phone him at home. I really couldn't have blamed him if he'd given me a right old telling off, or hung up, but on the contrary, he was extremely helpful and friendly.

However, it is rather fitting that, 27 years later, when I rang a different number and asked again to speak to Roy, but this time in connection with this book, I suddenly had a strange feeling of deja vu, and a memory returned to me of a long forgotten incident in a phone box in Moreton...

During the winter months, not long after the station's launch, a competition was run which was potentially risky for the station, and one that I really cannot imagine being undertaken in the same way today.

'Scully' was an hour long programme that went out between 10 am and 11 am every Sunday morning. It was written and presented by Alan Bleasdale, a one-time teacher who was already a brilliant and respected local writer, but still a few years away from the fame he was to achieve nationally with dramas such as The Black Stuff and GBH. 'Scully' was produced by Robert Cooper who went on to become a noted BBC TV and Radio 4 drama producer, as well as the producer of movies such as 'Truly Madly Deeply', and also head of drama in Northern Ireland. Gillian Reynolds remembers how it all started. "Alan had done some short stories for Radio Merseyside and his Studio Manager there, Robert Cooper came to me with the idea of a fictional disc jockey; Alan being Franny Scully, to be produced by him. We agreed it and our company secretary, Norman Noonan, drew up the contract: Alan would write, present and permit one repeat each week for £75."

Franny Scully, you may recall, was an underachieving schoolboy from Liverpool who was obsessed with Liverpool Football Club. His only dream was to play for them and his hero was Kenny Dalglish. There were records played within this show, but the reason most of us tuned in, myself included, was to hear the wonderful scouse wit of Scully's anecdotes. Despite having to suspend disbelief at the voice which supposedly came from the mouth of a 15 year old but sounded more like his Dad, as it was Alan himself, it not surprisingly became one of Radio City's most popular programmes. On 3rd January 1978, the character Scully graduated to BBC1 when 'Scully's New Year's Eve' was broadcast at 9.25 pm as part of the Play For Today series with Andrew Schofield playing the part of the young scally hero.

Then one week a competition was run as part of Scully's show in which the prize would be to read the news on Radio City. Listeners were invited to send in cassettes of themselves, and Howard Hughes, a 16 year old schoolboy from Bootle was the eventual winner. "I was very shy about sending a cassette in and almost didn't, but was amazed to get a handwritten letter telling me I had won." said Howard. "I became a hero at school overnight!"

Before I go any further, I know that anyone reading this who remembers hearing Howard Hughes back then will be shocked by two things: firstly that he was so young, and secondly that he came from Bootle. The voice apparently, as Howard himself freely admits, had always been 'different'. He sounded like someone who would have read the news in the 1940s and he also sounded much, much older than his years. In fact, DJ Simon Tate recalls attending an Ideal Homes Exhibition in Aintree with Howard, and a small crowd of middle-aged women appeared who had turned up purely to see Howard. Apparently they were quite disappointed when they discovered how young he was!

But anyone who heard him would never forget him. I am certain that Sharron and I weren't the only 194 listeners who tried hard and yet failed to perfectly imitate that amazing voice – the fact that we were female never put us off! And as for the wonderful rhyming couplet "This has been Howard Hughes with Radio City news" well, it was a producer's dream. This boy would clearly go far.

Howard says "I recorded my piece at the studios on 28th November 1974 with Alan Bleasdale and his great producer, Robert Cooper. My parents dropped me off and went off to Owen Owen and George Henry Lee to shop."

But it wasn't an easy ride. Obviously at 16, Howard had no real experience of studio work. His only contact with the Stanley Street Studios up until then had been far less dramatic. "I first visited as a schoolboy" Howard remembers. "I walked in off the street and was in the newsroom, upstairs, before I was spotted, handed a car sticker and sent on my way... nicely."

Having become a celebrity overnight at his school, Chesterfield Road Comprehensive in Crosby, he suddenly found things very different as he was propelled into the adult world and he was understandably a little over-awed.

With just a hint of embarrassment he admits he brought his own sandwiches in on his first day and ate them in the park rather than go to the pub or wine bar with the other members of staff.

However with hindsight, Howard admits that he was being given the chance of a lifetime not just on a plate, but on a gilded platter. "I joined the

The Heart of Liverpool

station at 11 am one day, read a voice-piece into a bulletin at 12, and read the news all afternoon. This sort of thing doesn't happen any more." And Radio City did indeed invest a lot in Howard. The station paid for him to train as a journalist at Cardiff University. Along with this, they also sent him to be trained at Radio Clyde. "Years later, when I was at Capital Radio, I went up to Glasgow to train them!"

One of his greatest memories was when as a boy trainee he broke the news of John Lennon's death to a shocked Liverpool. "I was on the breakfast news shift during my leave time from University. I thought they'd take me off the air that day because it was such a huge story - they didn't."

It wasn't just the DJs who had fans either. Howard recalls "If you were on City you got great exposure; everyone heard you. I will never forget my first ever 'fan' card from the girls at the Medici Galleries shop on Bold Street. I sent them the only photo I had - a copy of my graduation picture! It stayed in the shop for years. I couldn't believe some people had taken the time to write to me."

Howard picked up a few nicknames along the way: 'White Knuckle' because he was so scared he gripped the back of the seat in the studio and the dubious-sounding 'Hard Hughes' which was, I hasten to add, for no other reason than that was the way he pronounced his name back then. For those of you who haven't heard him since those heady days of the '70s, I can reveal that his distinctive voice now sounds much more natural. I wondered why this was. "Twenty odd years is a long time" he says. "I've had the rough edges knocked off, and grown up. I was a boy back then. I smoothed out parts of it, you had to be neutral back then. But I think I went WAYYY too far at the beginning. These days what you hear is me, thanks to a man at Radio Clyde who said to me 'just be yerself laddie, you're fine as ye are!'"

1976

Brian Cullen, early 194 promotional photograph

In the summer of 1976, I finally discovered Radio City for myself. I was still under the impression that, as a commercial station, it wasn't very good. Well, it was implied although never actually stated but BBC radio stations 2 and Merseyside were always on the dial at home.

Then one day whilst visiting a friend's house, we were messing about in the kitchen when the radio blasted out that wonderful Top Of The Hour News Jingle. It would have been the first time I'd heard it. My friend, after having sang along with it rather badly, told me that Radio City was a great station, her favourite and that she listened all the time. Nothing further was said on the matter, but I had become subtly aware that someone actually listened and thought it was good.

I knew that the station ran 24 hours a day. That I did find rather fascinating because I imagined the guy in the dimly-lit studio at 3 am talking to listeners and playing music. What would he play? Who would be listening? It all seemed rather magical and romantic to me back then.

The Heart of Liverpool

Then without warning I became depressed. It was the summer break between changing schools. That may have had something to do with it because I was leaving all my friends behind to travel to a school where I would be miles away from home and knew no one. I certainly wasn't happy, but the depression brought accompanying insomnia. Suddenly staying awake throughout the night seemed much less of a magical thing. The hours dragged. I read books, but they made me feel worse. Every sentence I read seemed to hold some subliminal message which terrified me even more.

After a week or so of this torture, I began to think more and more of Radio City. Surely listening throughout the night would help it pass more quickly, and it might even be enjoyable. However, I didn't want to wake my parents; I was scared they wouldn't allow me have a radio on at night, but once I had come up with this idea I couldn't get it out of my head. It was time for action. I crept downstairs and into the kitchen where the portable radio was kept. I remember it well. It had a lurid green vinyl casing with a silver front and dials. I carried it upstairs and placed it beside my bed, being careful to close my bedroom door quietly. With the volume down very, very low I switched it on and began to search around for 194 Radio City. I found it eventually and I climbed back into bed and, hardly daring to breathe, began to listen.

The programme was 'Night Owl' and the DJ, I soon discovered, was Brian Cullen. I can actually remember some of the records that were played that night - '15 Bars' by the Stylistics, 'Shannon' by Henry Gross, but what intrigued me most about Night Owl was the strange muzak which made up the majority of the show's musical content.

Brian Cullen worked at Radio City between March 1976 and 1979, at which point he changed direction, going into selling and PR work. He had applied three times to work at 194; twice unsuccessfully, but it was third time lucky when he managed to get in thanks to David Maker, who had heard him on Radio Merseyside where he had managed to secure a job covering holidays and relief work on programmes such as 'The Billy Butler Show'. Once at City, David Maker was determined not to lose another of his through-the-night jocks and gave Brian a specific contract to cover Night Owl on the Thursday, Friday, Saturday and Sunday shows. Mark "Joenz" - a new boy himself back then, and clearly one with spelling difficulties - covered Monday, Tuesday and Wednesday.

It would be many years before I would discover that the strange muzak wasn't actually Brian's bizarre musical taste, but songs from the 'Canadian Talent Library' which was used by Radio City to help fill the gaps left by

194 Radio City

Needletime restrictions. In fact the use of records was still restricted quite heavily in those days and both the BBC and commercial radio stations had to resort to finding their way around these restrictions, usually by broadcasting live music if possible, or by using film soundtracks, or quite often the bank of records from the Canadian Talent Library.

The Canadian Talent Library Trust, or CTL as it was more commonly known, was a non-profit trust that produced a series of recordings between the years 1962 and 1985 by Canadian artists and of Canadian compositions. Although a few great names started off on there such as Gordon Lightfoot, who would become one of my all-time favourite singer-songwriters, the majority of the music was middle-of-the-road, boring, uninspired covers - often instrumental - of popular songs from over the years. I have recently discovered that CTL has built up quite a cult following and, if you so wish, you can still buy your own recordings of the stuff - there are 268 LPs to choose from.

Of course Needletime restrictions were difficult enough to work around on regular radio stations that closed down overnight, but Radio City ran for 24 hours a day. The restrictions specified that only nine hours of popular music could be played in any one day. Understandably, Radio City wanted to spread the majority of that nine hours over the daytime, so it was poor Night Owl that suffered the most, having most of its musical output as CTL and similar.

Because of this, as you would imagine, Brian remembers CTL only too well, but says that after a while, he got wise to the fact that none of the management were actually listening through the night, so he used to bring his own stuff in. There was a spot called 'Night Break' where station staff would bring in tea and coffee and play their own favourite records. Sounds like fun and a bit of a doddle, but it could be a pretty dismal job to do night after night. There were only two turntables in the studio and Brian would usually have to work thoughout the night alone, with no engineer. If one of the turntables broke down, Brian would have to phone Chief Engineer, Peter Duncan, at home and get him out of bed to come and fix it. Other than Brian, there would only be the security guard in the building. Also, the toilets were two floors up from the studio, so if he took a break and the record stuck, he would have to hurtle back down himself to put things right. And of course Brian, like everyone else who worked in the original studios, had heard the rumours that the place was haunted.

The studios where Radio City would broadcast from were housed, as every fan knew, in nos 8-10 Stanley Street. Prior to work commencing, the building was little more than a shell, which had formerly been a warehouse.

The Heart of Liverpool

The rooms no longer possessed any architectural features to speak of and were, in effect, a huge blank canvas on which Radio City could stamp its very individual mark. But along with the elderly building, came the obligatory ghost. Or ghosts. Because depending on who you talk to, the stories change. Many of the people who worked there claim to have seen it.

Mark Jones: "The bloody ghost! I don't actually believe in ghosts, but... In the 19th century a guy was killed when he fell down the lift shaft. He's supposed to walk the building at night. "Cobblers!" said a very cynical Mark. But why, when there were only two of us in the building - myself and Bert the old security guard who I could see in the reception area - did my cup of coffee keep moving around the studio. As did some of the records eh? Hmmmm."

Paul Leckie: "There were two spirits: Patsy and Margaret. The story goes that Patsy killed herself down one of the old lift shafts in the then Stanley Street Warehouses after she was jilted by her lover. I'm not sure where Margaret came from. These spirits lived on the third floor by the kitchen and toilets. Many female newsreaders would not venture up there on their own at night.

"There were several 'cold spots' throughout the building and I experienced an entity one night at about 12.30 am. I was presenting 'The Peaceful Hour' on 'Downtown' in the dark when the studio door in front of me flung open violently, followed by a large white transparent cloud which then flung open the other door leading to reception and then left. The studio turned icy cold.

"I nearly freaked out and went out into reception - no one was there. I turned all the lights back on. Bob, the security man, came in 20 minutes later. I was shaking and asked if he had been in the studio. He said he had been on the second floor doing his rounds and that there was no one else in the building.

"For several months, I left all the lights on and wouldn't present in the dark!"

Brian Cullen, much to his relief, didn't encounter the ghost. And despite the strange musical content and the possibility of technical problems, in the very early days I thought Brian Cullen was just the best thing. He sounded so friendly and at last I could get an idea of the people he was talking to as he read out requests for lorry drivers, night watchmen, jobless and plain old insomniacs like myself. It was like another secret little world out there that continued while everyone else slept, and I adored it. It was a scene straight from a Harry Chapin song, although I didn't know this at the time! And it became my world too. I was completely hooked, and Night Owl became my companion throughout most of the nights that summer. It was so good in fact that, inevitably, I began to fall asleep before the show ended as the insomnia and ultimately the depression passed, all thanks to Brian and his muzak.

A Musical Education

Of course, I still had to go to the new school in September, and sadly this put a stop to me listening to the radio throughout the night, although as I was now a City addict, I simply switched to Downtown - the 10 pm till 2 am show - and tried to catch the first hour of Night Owl as well.

The school, Oxley Senior Comprehensive School in the middle of the Leasowe Estate, was every bit as bad as I had imagined it would be. The building was a tired, run down, unattractive sprawling thing consisting of one main building and various prefab huts dotted around. The teachers were strange characters to say the least and there was I, thrown into a class with thirty or so other girls, most of whom knew someone there. I knew no one. Not one of my friends or acquaintances had followed me here. It was a pure fluke I ended up at Oxley in the first place. Back then there were three high schools to choose from. In the last year of your middle school, parents received a form on which to put their order of preference. No one wanted to go to Oxley, at least no one from Poulton where I lived. My mother put the other two schools down on the list, omitting the name of Oxley completely to indicate just how strongly I did not want to go there. It didn't matter though, that's where I was sent by the school authorities, and on day one I was still reeling from the shock and unfairness of it all. I could have walked to either of the other two schools on the list, but to reach Oxley, I had to catch a bus and was given a bus pass because it was so far away. A sensible decision by the school authorities then.

However, as so often happens, I eventually settled in to the routine, certainly not happily but then, what choice did I have? Sharron Hendy was another girl in the class with apparently no particular friends, so naturally we gravitated towards each other. Most surprisingly I was to discover pretty quickly that not only did she love music as much as I did, but she also was a big fan of Radio City. She already owned photographs of a few of the DJs and it was here at school that I first saw the faces behind some of the voices when she brought the pictures in. I was impressed too because she knew more about the station and had been listening longer than I had, having the advantage of parents who liked the station themselves and listened in the day. Mine, unfortunately, stuck rigidly to the BBC. Although they now knew of my secret bedtime habit and tolerated me keeping the radio beside my bed, City was NOT to be played downstairs - God forbid! I was determined to work on them though.

194 Radio City

So the bond was formed between Sharron and myself. Then after the first year of simply listening to the station, moving on to collecting signed photos, car stickers and such by writing in to PO Box 194 in Liverpool, Sharron casually let it slip that she knew where the Radio City studios were. I think she had been past them on a shopping trip to Liverpool with her mum and dad. We discussed how it would be fun one day to go over there to see if we could spot any DJs as they arrived and departed the studios.

In 1977, Radio City started to run the regular summer roadshows. And I am proud to report that I was there at the very first one, along with Sharron and another friend, Vickie. There was a brand new red and white lorry with a matching pristine stage attached and with the Radio City logo and signs adorning it. It may have been summer in name, but the weather was bitterly cold and windy and to make it even worse, the inauguration

The first Radio City Roadshow at Liverpool's Pier Head, 1978
DJs are Mark Joenz (front) and Dave Eastwood (right)

took place at Liverpool's Pier Head, never the warmest of places. Nevertheless, it was a fantastic experience. The DJs who hosted the roadshow that day were Mark Joenz and Dave Eastwood who proudly displayed their new matching Radio City jumpers with their names on them. These jumpers were seen regularly in DJ photographs of the 1970s, and they were hand-made by Norman Thomas's wife. There were games, competitions, lots of music with requests, opportunities to get autographs and a little shop towards the rear of the van where you could buy Radio City

The Heart of Liverpool

memorabilia. I bought a Radio City patch that day which I begged my mum to sew on to my jeans later on. It went well with the 194 T shirt - another recent purchase from PO Box 194.

From 1978 onwards, the Radio City Roadshows had become a regular summertime jaunt, transport courtesy of Sharron's parents if they were too distant. Here, apart from the DJs, we could also see other local celebrities - bands such as The Real Thing and Liverpool Express. Well attended, yet still providing Sharron and me with enough opportunity to chat to the DJs and pass on our requests, hardly a week now went by without one of us, usually both, getting some mention or other and a favourite record played on Downtown.

The author, DJ Chris Jones and friend Sharron at the St Helens Show 1978

During these roadshows we had become aware of a group of three girls who, like us, were clearly DJ spotters. We wouldn't have given them a second thought except for the fact that we began to notice that whenever a DJ spoke to either Sharron or me, one or more of these girls would be giving us looks that shot daggers. We referred to them between ourselves as 'The Blanket Coats' as that was their usual attire. Whenever I worry that I may have been bordering on the sadly obsessive in those days, I remind myself of the time when these girls turned up to the St Helens Show, minus their coats for once, in Radio City T Shirts which had been signed by various DJs. Bad enough you might think, however to our amusement when we looked closely it became apparent that these girls had obviously spent many a long hour of devotion. They had lovingly, and very neatly, embroidered over every single name!

After one of the early roadshows which had taken place over in Liverpool, Sharron suggested we go to Stanley Street and she would show me where the studios were. How wonderful to see 8-10 Stanley Street for the first time. It was Mecca to me! There was the logo on the sign hanging proudly outside the door and you could just make out people moving around inside. We decided to stand on the opposite side of the road, sheltered within the doorway of a solicitor's office. From here we would have a perfect view of the comings and goings. Although it wasn't planned at the time, this was to be our vantage point for at least a couple of years. We'd take the trip over once or twice a month, catching the ferry from the Seacombe terminal and then walking up Water Street and Dale Street before finally turning on to Stanley Street. After a good day DJ-spotting, we would usually traipse over to W H Smith to peruse the latest LPs. I think this was where our fascination for all the information on the back of LP covers came from. Not being able to afford every album we craved was a big issue for us, but we could read all about who was involved on the back of those LP covers. Not just the session musicians but also arrangers, producers, photographers etc. We learned quite a lot from W H Smith in those days.

Sharron had an older brother, Malcolm, who was heavily into prog rock and getting the perfect stereo sound, and he would mock our cheap, tinny little record players. However Sharron and I were adamant that any money we had should go on actual music, rather than updating our players. There was far too much music out there and to spend any little money we had on equipment would mean missing out on much desired LPs. And that would be ridiculous! After all, we could enjoy the music when we first heard it through a little transistor radio, so it would be just fine coming from our hi fis. Actually, hi fi was too good a word for my record player. Popularly known as the 'Fidelity Mini Player', the HF42 was a portable, mono, red plastic thing, compact and lightweight - or so the sales pitch said - which did the job, except that when you played LPs, the arm would often catch on the record, causing it to slow down or, more alarmingly, rise up and wave around wildly before rejoining the LP, but whereabouts would be anyone's guess. My dad sandpapered the underside of the arm initially and that helped a little, but then I discovered that by carefully bending the 12" record before playing, I could reduce this unfortunate tendency. It was a

The Heart of Liverpool

risky business and I shudder to think of it today, but I only ever broke two LPs whilst undertaking this delicate operation - Billy Joel's 'The Stranger' and Chris de Burgh's 'At the End of a Perfect Day', both within about a month of each other, after which time I decided enough was enough, and requested a better record player for my next birthday, which I was lucky enough to get. This one, although better, ironically didn't last as long as its predecessor, because as soon as I started work, I quickly came round to Malcom's way of thinking and splashed out on the best system my money could buy.

But for the moment pleasures would have to remain simple and inexpensive. Standing in Stanley Street didn't cost anything of course, and eventually we even got to know a few of the DJs fairly well.

At the time, Stanley Street was full of parking meters and we soon realised that this was a good thing as far as we were concerned, because every so often people would have to pop out of the Radio City building to put money into the meters. Here they would often be accosted by us for autographs and maybe a little chat about their shows, music or something they'd said on air. Occasionally, requests for a record on a particular show would be handed over.

One of the strangest things we did in the early days of DJ spotting, was to compile a list of DJ's cars and their registration numbers. I still have this bizarre collection, I discovered recently, in the back two pages of an old autograph book. Rob Jones started the list. He had a distinctive blue Triumph TR7, so that is listed along with the reg LHF 658R. However, being girls, we obviously didn't know too much about cars, despite Sharon's dad working at Vauxhall's, so the listing quality deteriorates somewhat after this. For example, Chris Jones's is VCM 258L - yellow Ford. Brian Cullen just has a reg number VBG 430M, but no colour or make. Mark Joenz has a very tasteful sounding one: UFV 638K - Ford, black and red, black roof, with loads of stickers, and Phil Easton's is GTJ 289N - Ford? (sic) Red (ish). I don't think we'd have been much good as private detectives in those days, although the signs clearly showed potential for the future.

The memory has a natural tendency to play tricks, however it always seems to me, as I think back to those Saturday mornings outside the Radio City Studios that it was permanently raining and bitterly cold. We huddled together in that doorway opposite, watching, with our autograph books in hand, to see who would be next to exit those hallowed doors. DJs by now were instantly recognisable of course, however if it was an unfamiliar face we would take guesses as to who it might be - one of the newsreaders, perhaps?

194 Radio City

I don't know whether others kept this strange weekend vigil; we certainly never noticed anyone else. We must have been an amusing sight to those inside nos 8-10 Stanley Street - not to mention the other nearby establishments. However, without exception, the DJs we accosted on their way to their cars were always polite, chatty and willing to accept requests for their next show. The autograph books duly filled up, photographs were signed and we returned home happy - at least for another week or two.

Rob Jones - A Crazy Love

Rob Jones from an early 208 Radio Luxembourg promotional photograph, 1978

I loved all the Radio City DJs back in the early days, but Rob Jones became the only one on whom I developed what could properly be called a teenage crush. I would have been 14 or 15 years old at the time when I first noticed him on one of our Saturday mornings parked outside the Stanley Street Studios. He was only short but had a fun, perky personality, was very friendly and had a nice car - the brand new blue

194 Radio City

TR7 sports car. Let's be honest, it helped - even to my young eyes. Oh, and he was cute.

Rob had been at Radio City since its inception. Having only covered the basics on a course called 'Principles of Broadcasting' whilst attending the 6th form at Liverpool College, he was not exactly an experienced presenter. His tutor there, Ian Lightbody, had previously worked at the BBC and still had useful connections, so when Rob was 16 years old, Ian took him to see Alan Freeman presenting 'Pick of the Pops' at the BBC studios. Rob was hooked from then on. Having tried unsuccessfully to get into radio for quite some time whilst working as a trainee accountant in Liverpool's City Centre, he suddenly received three interviews in the space of one week: a studio engineer's job at Capital, the midday show at Piccadilly and presenter of Night Owl at Radio City. He was surprised to be offered jobs at all three, but decided to take the job at Radio City because he was still living at his mum's house and didn't honestly imagine that the job would last very long. However it did, and he went on to become a very popular DJ, especially with City's younger audience. Although he started off on the Night Owl programme, as did most novices, he also covered hockey for the sports news team, having been a local hockey champion. Pretty soon he was called on to cover the weekend Breakfast Show and the Top 40 show. Incidentally Rob now reveals that at the same time as the above job interviews, he also applied for a job at Radio Royal, the Liverpool hospital radio station, and was turned down! Unsurprisingly, he claims not to have been too upset about that.

Then in 1978 he was lucky enough to land a job at Radio Luxembourg. Tony Prince, who was at the time Programme Director at the station, as well as one of their top DJs, had heard Rob on his car radio whilst driving to visit relatives in Oldham. He thought he was so good, that he rang Rob to ask him to come for an interview. Peter Powell had recently left to join Radio 1 and there was a vacancy for a young, vibrant presenter. When Rob passed the interview and made the decision to leave Radio City, we in Liverpool were devastated, but it was rather exciting to see one of our own local DJs moving on to potentially greater things.

On one of his last weekends in Liverpool, Sharron, Debbie and I had travelled over for our usual Saturday morning DJ spotting, and were lucky enough to have quite a lengthy chat with him about his new job. He asked us whether we would continue to listen to him once he'd left Liverpool and I said I was unsure whether my prehistoric radio was able to pick up the signals from the Grand Duchy, but I'd certainly try. He asked us to write to him at Luxembourg and of course we agreed. He drove off after sadly

The Heart of Liverpool

confiding that he'd have to sell his beloved TR7 when he went. As we watched him go with heavy hearts, we discussed how much we'd miss him and wallowed in our collective loss.

It didn't seem long before he drove back down the road and pulled over laughingly saying "Are you still here?" Another brief chat and he was gone - this time for good. However, the fact that he'd come back left us all giggly and euphoric.

True to my word, I did write to Rob at Radio Luxembourg and, true to his, he wrote back some lovely little letters, signed 'love and lollipops,' and including signed photographs. "I hope you don't mind" he said in one "that I'm including one of my new 208 photos". Mind? I was ecstatic - he looked gorgeous, and up it went on the bedroom wall, along with my newly acquired Radio City DJ poster.

Our correspondence usually consisted of Everton (I was an Everton fan back then, as was Rob, and he occasionally came back and saw matches), Radio City (obviously), his car (I was pleased to discover he'd kept his TR7 and had it in Luxembourg with him) and what he was doing and places he was visiting. Then unbelievably, I learned that Rob had accepted a job on ITV presenting a pop show.

'Breakers' had only recently been commissioned, and was to be produced by Muriel Young. Muriel had worked on Radio Luxembourg herself many years before, but was better known for producing children's TV programmes such as 'Clapperboard', 'Lift off with Ayshea' and 'Shang-a-lang'. There were three presenters sharing the 'Breakers' series: Roy North, Paul Nicholas and Mark Bolan. Tragically, Mark Bolan died in a car accident just as the series began, and a new presenter had to be found very quickly. Lee Winstone, who was a plugger for Private Stock Records remembered having heard Rob on Radio Luxembourg and suggested Muriel give the job to him, which she did, much to my joy. I had to dash frantically home from school to see the show, and due to the appallingly slow school buses I only just made it. The pent up emotion was almost unbearable. I can remember crying my eyes out when he appeared on screen, much to the horror and disgust of my 11 year old brother, Chris, who was quietly sulking because he wanted to watch Blue Peter on BBC1.

Around this time, I began to buy the magazine Fab 208 regularly. This was a teenage magazine, which along with a problem page, 'true life' stories, fashion advice and pop star pin-ups, contained pages covering the latest Radio Luxembourg news. Rob would be in there pretty much every week, being groomed as the station's latest young heartthrob. Some of the headlines and stories which appeared were amusing, such as 'Rob - The

194 Radio City

Master Chef' (cooking Beef Paprika for the other Luxy DJs and their wives - and feeling a gooseberry!) 'The Fabulous Rob Jones Predictions for 1979' (most of them extremely silly, such as Prince Charles to marry Meg Mortimer from Crossroads, but one of the predictions is that pre-Live Aid Bob Geldof will become Prime Minister, hmmm interesting that one.) 'Rob to Marry in 1980' (a little worrying at the time) 'Rob's Pet Rock' (he takes it for a walk, but he gets funny looks and its collar keeps slipping off...) And a wonderfully teen-mag style interview with Michael Jackson (Rob: "What are your hobbies?" Michael: "My hobbies are looking at video tapes and reading. But my main hobby is watching people dance and talking to children. I love just being with children." Rob: "That's nice. Do you have a favourite TV programme...?")

Incidentally, Rob began working at Luxembourg at the same time as another young independent local DJ from Radio 210 Thames Valley - one Mike Read. As far as Rob's Liverpool fans were concerned there was no contest. Rob had it all - looks, personality, talent. Mike Read had nothing, yet incredibly, he was the DJ who made it to Radio 1 and became one of the country's top celebrity DJs in the 1980s. How I hated him. It seemed however, that Rob had set his sights on other things early on. He confessed in an interview in Fab 208 in 1979 that he didn't want to remain a DJ for ever and listed becoming an airline pilot, presenting Nationwide or Grandstand on TV, or perhaps being involved in professional football, were other things he might like to pursue. He even released a one-off single called 'Crazy Love' which unfortunately, I wasn't lucky enough to hear. Needless to say, it didn't exactly set the charts alight.   Except in one country. "It got to number 11 in Holland!" laughs Rob. There was talk of an album, but Rob says that if he is honest, he just wasn't good enough and that idea was quietly dropped.

Eventually Rob moved away from radio, turning instead towards the newly launched Sky TV. Interestingly, just before he took up this post, he received a telephone call from Terry Smith asking him to consider the post of Programme Director at Radio City. So Rob returned to Liverpool to chat with the City bosses, but in the end decided it wouldn't have been right for him at that time, and that there would be more opportunities in London with Sky. Having also worked for Virgin, Rob now he runs USP which is one of Britain's leading radio specialist marketing agencies and production companies.

Rob and I had continued to correspond well into 1979, until the day that a letter arrived from Luxembourg with an unfamiliar scrawl on the envelope. Up until this time, Rob had not only written the letters, but also the

The Heart of Liverpool

envelopes as well. Inside this one was a standard typed letter obviously sent to all fans. That was the end as far as I was concerned - unforgivable, and I never wrote to him again. Anyway, teenagers are nothing if not fickle. Ex-Radio Caroline star, Johnny Jason had started at Radio City and he was proving to be pretty good, and I was also becoming a big fan and friend of Rob's best friend at City, Dave Eastwood, who incidentally informed me of the real reason Rob still had the TR7 with him in Luxembourg; it kept breaking down and Rob couldn't even give it away. Was this true? I don't know, Rob's not saying!

Downtown

Downtown was my favourite Radio City show throughout all my listening years. I wasn't the only one. It was a request and dedication show and fast became compulsory listening to many. It broadcast between 10 pm and 2 am, and the most popular part of the show was 'The Peaceful Hour' which took place between midnight and 1 am. It had been given the name 'The Peaceful Hour' by Mark Jones when he covered the show during City's early years, but the name had stuck, and in fact it still exists, albeit in a more modern form today. Back then it played the most beautiful music, usually album tracks, and listeners were enthralled. In the middle to late 1970s, 'Tommy' by Dutch prog rock band Focus was The Peaceful Hour theme and when, following the midnight news, we would hear that drum roll and those first few notes of Jan Ackerman's guitar, we were immediately in the mood, hungrily anticipating whatever aural pleasure was to come.

Most DJs who covered the show have very fond memories of that time. "I think that Downtown evolved into the show it was because of the listeners at that time" remembers Chris Jones, who started off as an engineer at City, but soon moved into presenting, covering Downtown on and off from 1975. "The brief was originally arts orientated. We had to do stuff about ballet and theatre and classical concerts. That was under Bill Bingham. We even had Chas and Dave in to do live songs before they were famous. Melanie came in to do some live songs. She was nervous when not behind her guitar."

Downtown also had special features in the early days, such as one I particularly remember. It was Halloween and a hypnotist guested on the show who practiced regression. He sent a woman back to a previous life at the start of Downtown, and she was then interviewed, whilst under hypnosis, during the show. This unusual edition was interspersed with records such as 'Spooky' by the Atlanta Rhythm Section and 'Black Magic Woman' by Fleetwood Mac. Chris Jones was the DJ that particular night.

"The hypnotist was Joe Keeton who lived at Hoylake" says Chris. "His wife was features writer for the Liverpool Echo. I was hypnotised after the show and told I would never fall asleep behind the wheel of a car. I think its wearing off a bit, or perhaps I'm doing many more miles late at night now. He was the top guy on hypnotic regression and had written books on it. It is now recognised as a therapy. A friend of Dave Lincoln and myself went to see Joe and she was regressed. He identified a problem she had in

The Heart of Liverpool

childhood, made her relive it and after that she was a lot more confident and her career took off. So far as I can see it worked."

Mark Jones recalls the flexibility available to the DJs in City's early years, especially on Downtown. "In those days we could play virtually anything we wanted. So I used to wander into the studio with all my Who records."

And it wasn't always peaceful. Arthur Murphy, who covered Downtown in the early years remembers a particular incident when he was presenting. "I was doing Downtown when a posse of detectives and uniformed police suddenly appeared in the studio to inform me that they had received a phone call stating that a bomb had been planted in the studio to 'get rid of that Irish git on air'. So while I carried on broadcasting, they were searching the studio, even under my feet, for a bomb. To be fair, they told me it was probably some drunk coming out of a club who had made the call, but they couldn't leave the situation to chance. I had the commissionaire at the door ring Terry Smith, the Managing Director, as to what I should do, ie maybe get out. The reply was to carry on. That's how expendable a presenter was."

Arthur Murphy early 194 promotional photograph

Another Downtown memory which remains clear to Arthur concerned some of the people who wrote in for requests. "I was not only surprised at the number of listeners I had, but in particular the predominance of lonely women, especially those whose men were in Walton Jail. I used to play dedications for them, but never mentioned where they were, just residing at the Queen's Hotel, Walton, or just the postal number of the place. However

I was asked to stop doing it because the police were worried that the request might be coded messages to possibly help prison escapes."

I really enjoyed Arthur Murphy on Downtown, however, that pleasure was to be short-lived. In less than a year from the date I first discovered City, he was gone. Arthur had been travelling from Dublin to Liverpool and back every weekend, but it wasn't easy. "To begin with I used to fly back and forth but in 1974, the oil cartels put up the price of oil, and aeroplane tickets rocketed in price so I had to get on the ferry from Dun Laoghaire to Holyhead overnight and catch a train to Liverpool early next morning. As City management would not meet my travelling expenses and the Labour government at the time only allowed a yearly 10% increase in salaries per year, the whole process became an unviable proposition for me so I left in April 1977."

Johnny Jason was to become a long-term presenter of Downtown. He remembers his years there with great affection. "OK, so the hours weren't exactly sociable, however we had a load of dedicated listeners, who were not only into the music, of the laid-back variety, but turned the show into a very successful request programme, with The Peaceful Hour at midnight very much the highlight."

Dave Eastwood was another regular host of the weekend Downtown for quite a few years, and he brought his own inimitable style to the show. His son Richard remembers his Dad had a collection of around 10,000 LPs, carefully catalogued, which took up a whole room at home. Dave didn't bother with Radio City's vast record library, preferring instead to work out the running order for his show at home, and then bring his own records in. Dave's Peaceful Hour was much less soulful than other DJ's of the time. Still romantic, yet often more melancholy, it would include wonderful 'story songs' such as 'Corey's Coming' or 'A Better Place To Be' by Harry Chapin, and lesser-known gems from the likes of Neil Diamond, Bread and even Frank Sinatra.

Downtown's huge popularity was to last for many years, well into the 1980s. Paul Leckie couldn't believe his luck when he ended up presenting what had been his favourite show as a listener. "I had been in hospital radio since 1978 and when I landed the weekend Downtown slot from Simon Tate who moved to Red Rose, it was indeed a dream come true.

"Having heard a demo, Wally Scott, the then Deputy Programme Controller, called me for a five minute chat, asked me to do an hour of Night Owl, and the next thing I knew I was on Downtown and doing The Peaceful Hour on Friday night - it all happened so quickly.

The Heart of Liverpool

"The Peaceful Hour had always been my favourite part of the show. As a lover of romantic music, especially soul, The Peaceful Hour was heaven to me. In the 1980s I chose my own Peaceful Hour music which was brilliant. Favourite Peaceful Hour songs included 'Loving You' by Minnie Ripperton, 'I'm Not In Love' by 10cc, 'Always' by Atlantic Starr, 'Have You Seen Her' by the Chi-Lites, 'She's Out of My Life' and 'One Day in your Life' by Michael Jackson and 'No 9 Dream' by John Lennon. I remember splitting up with a girlfriend one time and presenting The Peaceful Hour reduced me to tears that night. I just had to play the records back to back!

"Wonderful Merseyside people wrote and telephoned for mentions for their loved and lost ones. It brought people together. I had the pleasure of being the first Peaceful Hour DJ to bring in the 'Lonely Hearts' section, finding Miss or Mr Right for the listeners. The mail bag was enormous. I doubt if The Peaceful Hour of today has the same impact as in the '70s and '80s. I remember my audience figures in the '80s at midnight was in the region of half a million and I received 350 letters, just for the weekend shows!

"With the 'lights down low' I was in heaven in the dark playing my favourite music to a huge, loyal audience. At that time there didn't seem to be anyone on Merseyside who didn't listen to The Peaceful Hour - such was the impact."

Another presenter who covered Downtown during the 1980s was Simon Tate. He began working on Radio City in July 1979, covering first Night Owl and from here was asked to cover what was then the station's second most listened to show, after The Breakfast Show. "I was incredibly lucky because at that time there was a technicians' strike on ITV and it was also in the days when BBC Radio 1 and 2 went off the air at 10 o'clock, so between 11 pm and 2 am I was the only one around to listen to. In fact it was calculated that I had 82% of the radio listeners in the Merseyside area at one point. Eventually I shared Downtown during the week with Paul Jordan. He did four nights and I did three. We got 700 letters a week, which was pretty good considering that I'd heard an interview with Peter Powell, who was then on Radio 1, where he said he used to get 1,000 letters a week, but they were a national station. Although I didn't start my show until 10 pm, I had to get in to the studios by 5 pm to open all my mail and go through all the requests. There was so much to do but it was good fun."

Downtown was to change its format during the mid '80s. Paul Jordan, who eventually moved on to work at BBC Radio 1, thinks this change was vital. "I was asked to take over Downtown from Kevin Curtis and I wasn't sure about this because at the time. I was homesick for London, and I knew that Kevin did six nights per week and I just wasn't prepared to do that." But David Maker, recognising Paul's popularity with the young listeners, wanted him on the show at any cost and so allowed him to do pretty much whatever he wanted. So Paul dropped the heavy, request-filled style. "Between the hours of 10 and 12 midnight, the music was young and funky. Then The Peaceful Hour stayed pretty much the same - requests were still a feature here - and between the hours of 1 am and 2 am it was back to the upbeat style again." As he'd been given the opportunity to make the show his own, Paul readily accepted five nights a week.

Paul states that he used to receive 300 letters every day, and had to arrive in the studio at 2 o'clock in the afternoon to sort out his show, and then didn't leave until 2 am, when Downtown ended. He created characters which he worked into his programmes, and although he didn't read out requests, he would play music by people he liked such as Duran Duran and then ridicule bands he disliked such as Japan, and the fans would write in to agree or complain. This type of feature became hugely popular. Paul remembers fans waiting outside the studio doors, (not me -by this time I was long gone!) and was booked to appear on every roadshow, such was his popularity.

But why was Radio 1 so interested in a DJ from an independent Northern station? The reason was simple says Paul, and it also proves just how popular Downtown was back then. "I had a high placing in the Smash Hits Top DJ poll and there was only one other DJ from a local station in there, Timmy Mallet. All the rest were big names such as Steve Wright, Mike Read etc." Such was the popularity of Downtown, its listener numbers could literally break a DJ into the big time.

The Obsession Grows

I became such a big fan of Radio City that my school haversack, an old, brown hessian thing from the Army and Navy Stores, had as its central motif a huge 194 logo, lovingly and perfectly drawn by me in felt tip, which I was soon to discover was an unfortunate choice as the colours bled when it rained. Surrounding the logo were the names of my favourite DJs and also the singer-songwriters and bands which took up so much of my time and money; ELO, Chris de Burgh, Justin Hayward and Harry Chapin to name a few. It was a little out of step with other haversacks at school which were adorned with bands such as Genesis, Led Zeppelin, Jethro Tull and Pink Floyd, which was somewhat strange because this, remember, was an all-girl's school! Not that I had anything against those particular bands but I knew where my loyalties lay and was proud to display them.

School and its dreary lessons continued and I knuckled down and surprisingly, under the circumstances, did well. Except that is in maths.

I have never enjoyed nor understood maths no matter who tries to explain it to me. I have now given up all hope of ever understanding, and am just grateful that I live in the age of the calculator. But back then, I still held on to the forlorn hope that one day it would just 'click'. Despite my serious eagerness to learn, I was nonetheless hopeless and for maths lessons only, was placed in what can only be described as a 'remedial' class. Most of the girls didn't give two hoots about trying to understand what was going on and simply mucked around for the whole lesson, throwing things at or taking the mickey out of each other or the teacher and being plain obnoxious. As a consequence, myself and one other girl, Debbie, became star pupils just for making an effort. That's how I passed the exam and got a Grade 1 CSE. Not because of any mathematical prowess. Anyway, to get back to the point of the story, maths lessons were so boring and nigh on unbearable that both myself and Debbie brightened our time by decorating our desks with Radio City DJ photos. Yes, by this time I had managed to gather another willing subject to the fold and we had photos of Mark Joenz, Johnny Jason, Dave Eastwood, Rob Jones and Dave Lincoln around the desk. Purely as inspiration you understand. The teacher, bless him, who looked like he was heading for a nervous breakdown, tolerated these strange mascots, obviously not wanting to upset us by asking us to remove them and thereby provoking a riot from the remaining two well-behaved pupils. He even feigned interest and asked questions about them in a rather forced but friendly manner as he passed the desk.

194 Radio City

Debbie and I had to undertake the survey about people and their jobs prompting the phone call to Roy Saatchi, as you will recall. But for our CSE Maths coursework, we also had to conduct another survey of our choice and then show the results in graphs, pie charts etc. Our choice? Well, of course it was a survey conducted of 50 people about which radio station they preferred. Completely fabricated of course - couldn't be bothered to actually go out and conduct the research - and I think you can guess which station came out the winner. Anyway, as I said I did pass my CSE with a Grade 1, which was equivalent to an O level pass. Or so we were led to believe.... but that's another story. But for now, Radio City had come to my rescue once again.

City Talk

The Radio City Charity XI, including Kevin Keatings, Johnny Kennedy, Gary Bloom, Roy Kelly, Phil Easton, Mark Jones and Peter Booth. Also present is Derek Hatton, and stars of Brookside and Coronation Street

Of course as with any workplace, there have been some interesting and sometimes very funny stories connected with Radio City in the early years. We as listeners haven't been able to hear many of them, as they often concern things that went on behind the scenes.

Chris Jones recalls the night that Elvis died. "I was on air with Downtown when the newsman called down just as I had started, to say that there was an unconfirmed report that it had happened. It wasn't the first time there had been rumours of this kind but I dashed up to the record library and grabbed all the Elvis albums. It was soon obvious that Elvis had been rushed to hospital in a bad way and we tenuously started to speculate ourselves. It wasn't long before it was confirmed that the King was dead. I started ringing up all sorts of people to get a reaction. Everyone was in a state of shock. In the early hours I managed to contact the top radio station in Memphis, WMPS, they had a news car at the hospital and City listeners were able to hear their reporter giving the news of Elvis's death and quotes from the ER staff. The next night I ran a pulled-together hour of all the interviews we had done. I still have the tape of 'The Night that Elvis Died' at home. As I drove home that night I tuned across the medium wave and all the stations across Europe were playing Elvis songs."

Peter Levy began working at Radio City in December 1979. Until he moved on to Radio Aire in Leeds in 1981, he presented the weekday afternoon show, 'City Extra', with the exception of the occasional holiday relief on 'The Norman Thomas show'. He was brought in by David Maker after winning a radio award for Best Presenter. Having worked at a small radio station, he was quite unprepared for just how big Radio City was. He remembers being taken to a pub on his first day by David Maker and hearing all the scouse accents around him and feeling rather concerned, thinking "What have I done? I won't ever be accepted here with my voice." But he immediately felt at home. He remembers Billy Butler teasing him when he first walked into the studios by saying "What are you doing in a suit and tie? Did your mum get you ready?" and this type of banter continued throughout his time at City. Earlier on in his career, Peter had been an actor, appearing in programmes such as Dixon of Dock Green.

Many of the City Extra programmes would be scripted, usually by Mike Green of the news team, to take full advantage of the potential in particular interviewees, such as The Bee Gees or Rowan Atkinson. They proved very successful. Peter is still presenting and interviewing now, as part of the BBC's Look North magazine programme.

Peter remembers he interviewed many celebrities as host of City Extra: People such as Harold Wilson, David Essex, and Bill Shankly just two days before he died. He had previous experience of interviewing, but not to the extent he was now being given at City. He also recalls the day that John Lennon died. Peter was hosting City Extra that day and he held a phone-in. He recalls how people were phoning in in tears, while in the studio beside him, as the show was broadcasting, a US film crew were filming his show so those in the States could see what was going on in Lennon's home town.

Joe Butler who most famously hosted 'Country Style', Radio City's country music programme, had a very loyal audience who liked to look after him. "When I was doing 'Sunday Requests' I was always talking about my favourite Sunday dinner: roast beef and Yorkshire pudding. One Sunday, a listener brought down to the studios a full Sunday dinner of roast beef and all the trimmings, and guess what? That week it was a recorded show, and I wasn't there! Bert, our security man, had great pleasure in telling me about it the following week and how he had scoffed the lot!"

The Heart of Liverpool

In 1983 Johnny Kennedy joined the station. He was later to be known affectionately as JKJD.* "I had won 'New Faces' on television at about the same time Tom O'Connor won 'Opportunity Knocks'. In fact we appeared together at the Royal Festival Hall in London. This led to theatre, cabaret, and summer seasons throughout the UK. Then my agent, Ricky McCabe told me that Radio City were looking for a new presenter, but he had to be from Liverpool. This was at the end of 1983. Ricky arranged a meeting with Wally Scott at a little restaurant in Dale Street, and Wally said 'I hear you're doing great things in the clubs with lots of Liverpool material, do you think you could do it on the radio?'

"I said I was sure I could, so he arranged for me to come in and do an audition. The following evening I went down to Radio City in Stanley Street and did the audition in a little news studio at the top of the stairs. Wally played the records and told me to start talking as each record finished. He recorded the audition and said it had gone really well and he'd let Roger Wilkes, the Programme Controller, listen to it in the morning. I went home thinking that will be the last I'll hear of that, but early the next morning Wally rang me and asked me to come down right away. I met Roger Wilkes and he said he'd loved the tape, and had taken it upstairs for the boss, Terry Smith, to listen to and they were offering me a contract for a trial period of three months."

It wasn't always plain sailing though.

" I first went on air at Radio City in February 1984." recalls Johnny. "All these years later, with the knowledge of the radio industry I have acquired, I realise that my radio debut was very unusual. I came straight out of the theatres and clubs, with no radio experience and was given a peak time show on a major station.

"Obviously there was no way I could 'drive' the programme, so at first Brian Smart was brought in to drive for me, and after a while he was replaced by Tony Newman, who was Head of Music and had his own office on the first floor overlooking Stanley Street. I liked Tony; I thought he was a good guy. But I have to tell you that he wasn't pleased about having to drive for me, and he was quite right. He had his own job to do.

---

* The name came about as the result of an on-air slip-up. Johnny had been on air for about two weeks and was telling the audience how he couldn't believe his luck being paid for having a laugh and playing his favourite records. He'd meant to say "It's great being a DJ," but it came out as "Its great being a JD" and it just stuck. From that moment on he was 'JKJD', even receiving letters addressed simply to "JKJD, Liverpool."

194 Radio City

"After a couple of months of driving me, he stood up one day and said 'Right JK, I'm off now, you know enough about the desk to drive it yourself.' And with that, he walked out of the studio. And that's how I started driving my own show, and that's how I learned what all presenters know: it ain't your show until you can drive it.

"The next few months were amongst the most interesting in Radio City's history, as I found new ways of causing technical mayhem in the studio, and turned 'dead air' into an art form. My producer, the great Wally Scott, was like a Premiership goalkeeper as he leapt across Studio One to close faders I'd left open, or to press the cart machine at the start of an ad break. And one day after interviewing my old mate Bernard Manning on the phone, I pressed the wrong button and he couldn't use his phone for the rest of the day!

Tony Snell and Johnny Kennedy in the early 1980s

"Roger Wilkes, City's Programme Controller in 1984, was the man brave enough to give me my chance when Wally Scott brought me to his notice. Roger was very helpful to me in my early days, but I must have severely tested his patience with my technical ineptitude. Oddly enough, the listeners seemed to love it, and it almost became part of my style. To this

The Heart of Liverpool

day there are thousands who remember the 'acker macker valve'. If we had a bit of dead air or a record at the wrong speed, I'd say the 'acker macker valve' was knackered.

"Then came the fateful day when Wally Scott's nightmare became a reality. Radio City went off the air, and guess who was broadcasting at the time? Yeah, it was me.

"It was just coming up to midday so as a record ended I closed my fader, pushed the button on the news jingle cart, and put the news booth on air. Or thought I did. Nothing happened, so I played the news cart again. Still nothing, and by this time Ruby Williams, the newsreader, was waving frantically through the news booth window asking why she wasn't on air. By this time, we'd had about 30 seconds of dead air and in radio terms, that's a very long time indeed. Ruby rushed into the studio: 'What have you done?'

'Nothing!'

'Nothing? You must have done something, we're off the bloody air!'

"We had now had a minute of dead air which is the equivalent of about four years in real life. All I could think of was that I'd accidentally dislodged something under the desk with my foot, so I scrambled around on the floor and Ruby was running round shouting, when Roger Wilkes came into the studio and said 'Where is he?'

'He's under the desk.' said Ruby.

'Under the desk? He'll be more than under the desk when I get hold of him. He's put the bloody station off the air!'

At this point Phil Easton came through the door. Phil was one of my best mates at City, always an ally, and he tried to calm things down. 'What was the last thing you did J before you played the news jingle?'

'I just closed my fader.'

'Closed your fader?!' shouted Roger 'You just closed your fader and now we've been off-air for nearly 5 minutes!' For once in my life I was speechless, but I could already see the headlines in the Echo: JK SACKED FOR PUTTING CITY OFF THE AIR.

It was bedlam in the studio now with everyone rushing around and shouting, except for me. I was just standing there seeing the job I loved disappear out of the window.

At this point, the studio door opened and in walked Radio City's Chief Engineer Peter Duncan, cool as a cucumber.

'You took your time' said Roger.

'I have to inform you' said Peter 'that for the last 5 minutes, Radio City and selected radio stations throughout the country have been put off the air as part of our union's ongoing dispute. The action is now over and the station is back on the air.'

"I have never been so relieved in my life. After all the shouting and rushing around, and all the abuse hurled in my direction, it turned out that I was innocent. It wasn't JK who put Radio City off the air...

They did it themselves!"

Despite all this, the huge popularity of Johnny Kennedy's programmes on Radio City is highlighted by the fact that he won the Whitbread Radio Personality of the Year Award three times in the mid-80s and early '90s.

"I've heard people say, with false modesty, that awards don't mean anything to them" says Johnny. "Well they certainly meant a lot to me! And in the '80s and '90s they were genuine awards because voting slips appeared in the Liverpool Echo and the people chose the winners. I'm proud that on my awards it says 'Voted for by the people of Merseyside'"

Out of all the programmes Mark Jones has presented over the years for City, he found The Breakfast Show the easiest "probably" he says "because being teetotal, I never woke up with a hangover."

However for others, The Breakfast Show was a nightmare. Arthur Murphy, the original breakfast guy, was asked back to present The Breakfast Show on the occasions of Radio City's 5th and 10th anniversaries. "And I was no better getting up at that unearthly hour to do it than I had been when I was the first man on air in 1974" he admits. "I was always somewhat worried about not getting up in time which resulted in not sleeping very well."

Other presenters slept too well. Brian Cullen remembers when the late Roger Blyth presented The Breakfast Show. "I was covering Night Owl in the early years when Roger Blyth, who at that time lived in Heswall, was doing The Breakfast Show. I would have to ring him at 20 to 5 to wake him up. Roger would answer the phone very sleepily and say that he was on his way. But quite often he'd just go back to sleep again and it was only at 10 to 6 when he wasn't in the studio that I would realise and have to phone him again." Despite what one might imagine, this was actually quite beneficial to Brian, because he was then able to cover the beginning of The Breakfast Show, thereby gaining more exposure than he would have done by simply covering the through-the-night slot.

Roger Blyth of course went on to host 'Granada Reports' on television. It was many a DJ's dream to make the transition from radio to TV. One such dreamer was Norman Thomas. An anonymous insider reveals it was an open secret that Norman regularly tried to make the move to TV work in the early years of 194. And it appeared one day that his dream had come

The Heart of Liverpool

true when on returning to work via reception, he was told that he'd received a call from Granada TV. Norman could hardly contain himself and excitedly phoned the number on his desk. However it soon transpired that the caller was actually from Granada TV Rentals, who wanted Norman to preside over the opening of a new store. Never mind Norman, their loss was our gain!

Michael Green of the news team, recalls the time that David Maker, and most of Radio City's staff, were taken in by a fake sheikh. Allegedly a certain Sheikh Shubtill had contacted the station saying that he wished to set up a station in Saudi Arabia and he was impressed by Radio City which was really big at that time, and wanted to chat with the staff and come in and see how the station worked. He turned up in a chauffeur driven white Jaguar, and certainly looked the part, and was shown around the studios and taken for lavish meals by Maker, until one day, Peter Gould, who was a cryptic crossword addict, said "You do realise that 'Shubtill' is an anagram of 'bullshit' don't you?" The room went quiet, David Maker went white and dashed out of the room. After some investigation, it turned out that the 'sheikh' was a well-known con-man who, it is alleged, had decided to play a trick on the station because the voice of one of the DJs had been irritating him. History unfortunately does not reveal who that particular DJ was. David Maker actually forbade anyone to mention it for a while. Unfortunately for him, the story somehow made it to the front page of one of the national tabloids.

Radio City could be the joker too, and would often trick listeners with April Fool's Day jokes. Kieran Devaney recalls one particular time when the news revealed that 30,000 people were gathered at the Pier Head and traffic jams were building up around the City. It was the day the Mersey ran dry.

"Radio City's outside broadcast began at 7 am with Norman Thomas setting the scene from the Pier Head. A lecturer in Maritime Studies from Riversdale Tech. explained how the rare alignment of Jupiter, the moon and the sun would lead in a few short hours to the lowest tide for 785 years. People would be able to walk from Liverpool to Birkenhead across the bed of the Mersey. Scousers listening at home heard DJ Phil Easton do just that, with a little help from a team of mountaineers from Liverpool University, who brought ropes and pitons to scale the river bank on the Wirral side.

"Derek Hatton and Sir Trevor Jones, in a rare gesture of political unity, were there to give their reaction. Deep sea divers and marine archaeologist, Bernie McDonald and I broadcast from a Piper Cherokee two thousand feet

194 Radio City

over the River. Bernie pointed out historical wrecks which were becoming visible for the first time in generations as the waters parted.

"Exiled Scousers received hurried telephone calls from Liverpool as word of City's coverage spread from West Derby to the Dingle. In Birmingham a father bundled his wife and five kids into the car and drove to the Pier Head. Another family travelled from Leeds. A hotel owner in Mount Pleasant woke a party of twelve Japanese tourists and sent them down to the waterfront with cameras clicking.

"By nine o'clock that morning there was chaos on the buses and trains as Norman's warning that the tide was turning encouraged last minute sightseers to leave home.

"The next day newspapers as far away as America and India carried the story. 'The Miracle on the Mersey' proclaimed the Bombay Times, but the earnest reporter who telephoned the City newsroom from Bombay had realised what nearly all the people on Merseyside had forgotten. It was April Fool's Day. Humour was all part of the magic of working at Radio City."

Charity Raft race at Chester, February 1981, Johnny Jason (left centre), Phil Easton, (left, back) Ivor Godfrey-Davies, (right centre) Mark Jones (centre)

When I first chatted to Brian Cullen about his memories for inclusion in this book, he remembered that during his time at City, a friend had

The Heart of Liverpool

mentioned to him the fact that John Peel had played a record on his Radio 1 programme entitled '194 Radio City', which ended with some audio of Brian chatting on Night Owl. Brian was surprised as he'd had no idea that it existed. His friend had eventually managed to get hold of a copy for him, and Brian told me that he still had it on tape somewhere. The song was by two girls called Jaqui and Jeanette and the song concerned their falling in love with a late night DJ.

A few months later, I was out for lunch with a friend, Liverpool club DJ Mike Knowler, and we were discussing my Radio City research, and Mike revealed that he had a song about Radio City on an LP he had brought over to show me. The LP was entitled 'Street to Street - A Liverpool Album' and was a platform for upcoming new bands during the period May 1978 to May 1979.

I straightaway realised what the song was and discovered the amazing coincidence that Mike had actually produced the very album it came from. The song '194 Radio City' "...was conjured up during one of those all-star sessions that one reads about" wrote John Peel in the sleeve notes on the reverse of the LP. "Ian Broudie (later of the Lightening Seeds) wrote the song and plays guitar, Budgie (ex-Big In Japan and Slits, and later of Siouxsie and the Banshees) plays drums, Dave Balfe (ex-Teardrop Explodes) is at the keyboards, Ambrose (ex-Ded Byrds and Walkie Talkies and signed to Sire) mans the bass, and former Deaf School-er Steve Lindsey sings with Gary Dwyer, drummer with the Teardrop Explodes."

Mike (who was then known as 'Noddy' Knowler) recalls that the two girls who sang the lead, Jaqui and Jeanette, were not really singers at all, but simply two girls who "hung around the studios". So that was appropriate enough - they were obviously the vocal equivalent of Sharron and me then! When I asked Mike why Brian Cullen's voice had been chosen for the end of the record, he recalled that a guy who worked at the Open Eye studios, where the album was recorded, just happened to have a cassette of one of Brian's Night Owl programmes in a drawer, and so they all thought it appropriate to use that at the end of the song. Also featured on the LP are early ventures into music by Echo and The Bunnymen and Orchestral Manoevres in the Dark, who were then called 'The ID'. So Brian Cullen unknowingly got his chance to be up there recording with future '80s Indie music stars.

Home Thoughts from (not quite) Abroad

Mark Joenz in the original Studio 1, Stanley Street, 1976

Family holidays for us in the 1970s consisted of one week, usually Whit week, in Butlin's Holiday Camp, Pwllheli, North Wales. It was always Pwllheli, except for one year when we went a little crazy and tried Butlin's Skegness instead. However, the following year we were back at Pwllheli again. My mother hated driving and as the only driver in the family she claimed it would be no holiday for her if she drove us there and back, so instead we always travelled by National Express Coach. It took four tortuous hours with one toilet break and we always took plenty of plastic bags with us because invariably I was sick at least once on the journey.

Then in 1977 I had a brilliant idea. I would tape one whole night of Downtown and take it with me. This was clever on two counts. Firstly, Downtown was four hours long, so it would keep me amused for the whole journey, and hopefully my mind off the idea that I might soon meet my breakfast again. And secondly, as much as I loved Butlin's - and I really did;

The Heart of Liverpool

I used to cry uncontrollably and loudly when we had to return home, to the acute embarrassment of the rest of the family - Radio City had now become something I couldn't live without. The station signal wouldn't reach as far as Pwllheli, of course, and the idea of a whole week without City was unimaginable; cold turkey would surely have set in, so four hours of Downtown music with DJ Mark Joenz* hosting should be just enough of a fix to keep me going for a week.

This of course was before the era of the Walkman so once again out came my parents' trusty tape recorder with plastic shoulder strap, plug in microphone, and buttons the size of bricks and I set it up in front of the radio to record Saturday night and Sunday morning's Downtown on the weekend before we were to depart. After turning on the recorder I would dash out of the room so I didn't accidentally hear any of the show. I wanted to save that particular pleasure for the journey and the holiday. Actually, I still have bits of these Butlin's Downtown recordings to this day: the original Mark Joenz from '77 and a couple of Dave Eastwood ones from '79 and '80. Unfortunately the sound quality has deteriorated to virtually a whisper, but I wish I still had the whole shows even in this state because I taped everything; the news, adverts and jingles as well. They would be a marvellous slice of local history. Unfortunately, as I was on very limited pocket money back then, I couldn't afford to replace tapes or even add to the collection very often, so there were only six cassettes initially which were used again and again, year after year, if I was taping songs from the radio, requests and such like, so they all ended up a bit of a hotchpotch. But at least I have them, although I do feel like kicking myself sometimes when I listen to the fragments that are left. I remember feeling a little better when I learned that the BBC did a similar thing to its TV archives in the early years. At least I'm in good company.

Of course I couldn't just turn my tape recorder on and play it full blast on a coach load of holiday makers so I had to make do with an ear plug. And no, there were no dinky earphones in those days, instead all we had was a dreadful cream coloured ear plug which looked like a hearing aid and fitted into one ear. They were quite uncomfortable and of course stereo sound was impossible but it was better than the alternative (ie vomiting into a Kwik Save bag), although I remember after the journey I would remain deaf in one ear for the first day of every holiday.

* *Mark Jones initially chose to use the strange spelling of "Joenz" so that record company executives would remember him when he phoned them, and it did work. However, he found that it eventually wasn't required after about 1979 when record companies would come to see him. He made the final switch to his normal spelling when he had to make a decision as to how his name would appear on the side of a new car.*

Catching The Great Easton Express

The Great Easton Express, hosted of course by DJ Phil Easton, was the longest running specialist music show in all of independent local radio. At first, Radio City's 'Rock Show' was hosted by ex-BRMB jock John Henry, but after he left the station in 1975, Phil, was brought in to take over. Phil was a great fan of rock music and couldn't believe his luck to be hosting this particular show. He had been prepared to host any show at all - even the religious one - just to get into broadcasting, but was overjoyed to be given this already popular 6.30 pm to 9 pm rock slot.

The show didn't receive its distinctive name until 1976 when a competition was held for the listeners to find a more exciting name than 'The Rock Show'. Along with the new name and the famous jingle of the train pulling away from the platform as the station announcer lists all the surrounding areas which Radio City covered back then (including Blackburn, Llandudno, Wrexham, Chester and even Manchester), there was also a special T Shirt available briefly in the early days. This was emblazoned with the words 'The Great Easton Express', appearing as though they were carved from a large, heavy rock - appropriately - above the picture of an electric guitar with steam coming from it like a train. A much sought after rarity nowadays, even Phil no longer has one.

Although I did listen to the show fairly often, it was definitely accepted as being more of a lad's show. This wasn't strictly true. Sarah Smithard, who now works as the Managing Director of the Marcher Radio Group, was in her teenage years a big fan of Phil and his show. "My friends and I would listen every night and note down every single record that was played, and then phone each other up to discuss the tracks and see if we had missed anything" she says. She sheepishly admits, however that although she has worked in radio for over 15 years she has never met Phil Easton, has no idea what he looks like and knows that if she did meet him, she would be so nervous she would quite possibly pass out.

The rock element included a very wide range spanning prog rockers ELP to the more mainstream Dire Straits to, er, Chris de Burgh..... Chris de Burgh? Well yes. For those of you who came late to Chris, and by that I mean 'Lady In Red', it is hard to imagine, but back in those days, Chris rocked! He had become popular amongst Phil's audience when he had supported Supertramp on their 1977 tour. Chris played a live session on The Great Easton Express shortly after this and the phone lines were jammed with frantic callers desperate to speak to him (myself included - and

The Heart of Liverpool

yes, I did eventually get through!) Everybody at the station, and Chris's management were taken completely by surprise by his huge popularity in the Merseyside area and at the end of this particular show, it was revealed that Chris would be adding the Liverpool Empire to his current tour. Amazing!

I was there of course - front row, centre with Sharron... and my Dad. I was deemed too young to go to Liverpool at night alone, and had to be chaperoned. And even I now find it hard to believe that for the first few years that Chris played Liverpool, his audience consisted mainly of long-haired, leather-clad bikers/grebos/sweats/troggs (they had many tasteful names in those days) and their girlfriends.

Being a rock show, and specifically a 1970s rock show, it was not unusual for Phil to play tracks from bands that would go on for 20 minutes or more. This was unusual on radio stations in those days, except perhaps on pirate stations, and clearly City appeared to taking its lead in many ways from the pirates, when it came to music. It was certainly playing to the rock-obsessed youth of Liverpool and beyond. Again, listeners would write in to request favourite tracks, or sides of albums, and as could be seen in the example of Chris de Burgh above, the show could often break a band into the big time, purely if it received the right exposure on The Great Easton Express.

In 2005, despite the fact that it no longer exists, The Great Easton Express celebrated its 30th Anniversary, a year after the station's own 30th. The celebration was held in June at the Cavern Club in Mathew Street and featured live performances from some of Liverpool's finest bands from the past three decades. All proceeds from the tickets went appropriately to Radio City's own 'Give A Child A Chance' charity.

The Guitar Lessons

Bob Buckle today

Bob Buckle hosted Radio City's hour-long 'Folk Club' programme from the launch date until the late 1970s. He had previously worked on commercials at BRMB Radio in Birmingham, and had popped into the Stanley Street Studios prior to launch to see whether City required someone to do a similar job there. After a brief chat, Peter Duncan asked Bob whether he would be interested in hosting a folk programme, which he readily agreed to do, despite never having worked on a radio show before, and the rest, as they say, is history.

Bob has now been in the folk business for 40 years and has a rich musical heritage. Initially he was in a band called the Leesiders and went on briefly to join the Spinners with his brother-in-law Tony. He also has the honour of being the first person ever to sing live on Radio City. The song, for those of you interested in this sort of trivia, was entitled 'Burglar Man'.

Folk Club went out on at 9 pm on a Sunday evening, and was repeated at the same time on the following Tuesday. As a respected local folk singer, Bob's show would consist of his own songs and also recordings of folk music, old and new. For amateur guitarists such as myself and Sharron, it

The Heart of Liverpool

was ideal for gathering extra material such as the Jack Owen song 'Mist Over The Mersey' with which we, as budding folkies, could stun our non-existent audiences as we performed both on our own and as a duo in our bedrooms. Conveniently for us, at least, it was broadcast directly before Downtown, which made for a very good evening full of entertainment.

Bob was given a budget for his show, and he borrowed the outside broadcast van to travel around the local folk clubs to record live music, and he would often play host to big names on the folk circuit such as Alex Campbell and Bert Jansch, recording sessions and chatting about their music. Bob remembers they would be paid £15 for a ten song session. These were mini gems in their own right, but unfortunately they no longer exist. Bob takes up the story. "I had catalogued it all and put it in City's archives, and as far as I am aware it did stay there for nine months. But one day I went in to get one of the tapes and discovered it had all gone. Someone else had wanted the reels and had taped over them." Bob was devastated. Even his own personal diary from those years, he tells me rather sheepishly, which detailed every show he'd ever done and every musician he'd interviewed and who had recorded sessions, was thrown away only recently when he moved house and decided to have a clear out. So nothing remains of those days. That is if you discount a few snippets of very poor quality on my collection of Radio City cassettes.

Along with hosting Folk Club, Bob also ran his own agency. A lot of the sessions were recorded in the middle of the night at around 3 am when the studios were at their quietest. It was during this time that Bob recorded his first children's album when, following the sessions, Bob and an engineer would stay behind to record a song or two each time. Very generously, Radio City was also responsible for Bob getting his own 24 track studio installed in his house.

But Bob also had another sideline which was to become much more interesting to me following the demise of Folk Club.

I had fooled around with the acoustic guitar since the age of 10, starting off on one of those small, inexpensive ones, only one step up from a toy. My parents were obviously not going to spend a lot of money on something that they imagined would be quickly discarded as soon as I became frustrated with my lack of talent. But I thoroughly enjoyed it and was a regular attendee at the school's guitar club. Admittedly, not outstandingly talented but not too bad, I stuck with it as a favourite pastime for a number of years. Many of my evenings, when not listening to music, were spent working out the chord sequences to the songs I loved, and borrowing 'The

194 Radio City

Paul Simon Songbook' or 'Complete Beatles Songs' from other guitar playing friends.

Bob lived in Wallasey, as did I, and when I was about 16 years old I discovered that, along with recording and touring, he also made his living by giving guitar lessons. Actually, he had the reputation of being the best teacher in the area. Maybe I was setting my sights too high, but I dreamed of having the kudos that would come with taking lessons from an ex-Radio City presenter no less. Clearly too good an opportunity to miss - time to go cap in hand to the parents....

My mother unsurprisingly refused outright when asked if her and dad would help fund the lessons, pointing out that they were much too expensive. I was outraged - could my parents not see how important music was to me? They were preventing me from nurturing my budding talent! Hmmm who was I trying to kid? And anyway, they asked, why couldn't I go to somebody less expensive? Well, the reasons were obvious, of course, but wouldn't be classed as sensible to my parents. Such was the strength of my dream that I was eventually willing to fork out most of my earnings from my little Saturday job at the local Freeman Hardy Willis shoe shop on these lessons. My record buying would have to take a back seat for a while.

However, on phoning the Buckle household, my mother was informed that Bob was fully booked for the foreseeable future, although I could, if I wished, commence lessons with Bob's brother, Chris, straightaway while I went on a waiting list for Bob. After a brief feeling of disappointment and some consideration I agreed to this. After all, I would still be taking lessons at Bob's house and the lessons would undoubtedly be useful. I could prove to mum that I was serious, but the most important issue at this time was that these lessons would not be quite as expensive as the ones with Bob.

Chris Buckle was a very quiet and shy man. He was a competent teacher and I was an adequate pupil. That is all I know for sure. I can't remember exactly what I learned from him or how many lessons I had, but there weren't too many. I knew I still wanted to progress to the master. Eventually, I received the call that I could start lessons with Bob.

I can recall very clearly on that very first day sitting outside Bob's teaching room that doubled as a recording studio. Through the door, I could hear the last minutes of the previous pupil's lesson. I was suddenly extremely nervous, and not because Bob Buckle was an ex-Radio City presenter this time. In all the eagerness to become one of Bob's pupils I had forgotten one vitally important fact. Bizarrely as it may seem, I had made it a rule almost never to play my guitar in front of anyone, never mind sing. I

The Heart of Liverpool

realised now that this was going to be difficult, but not, I hoped, insurmountable.

I was eventually escorted into the room by Bob himself. It was fairly small with gleaming guitars and banjos displayed majestically around the walls. By this time, I had progressed to a shiny black lacquered satin jumbo acoustic guitar with twin hummingbird embossed scratchplates. I loved it. It had been an expensive purchase, in fact I was still paying for it on HP over 50 week terms, so imagine my horror when, on this first visit, Bob quickly looked over it and rather scornfully criticised its lack of quality. But I didn't care; I was here - I had achieved my ambition, and that was the most important thing.

I think I must have managed to fudge my way through Chris Buckle's lessons somehow without singing too loudly. I really can't remember, but Bob had a completely different style of teaching. He demanded a much more involved pupil and shyness wouldn't be accepted as an excuse here. To make matters worse, Bob used to record our weekly lesson in order for me to take it home and practice along with the exercises over the next seven days until I returned. Every week I sat there in the abject fear of having my voice or guitar playing recorded on that tape, so I barely uttered a word throughout the lessons.

Amazingly, despite all this, I took lessons regularly with Bob for about eight months and built up a nice little cassette library of songs and picking styles. In fact, I learned some fabulous tricks and, listening back to them now, I'm pretty impressed. I really can't remember being that good! Well, maybe I never really was *that* good because on one later lesson, Bob stopped me after a particularly poor recital that I'd been meant to be perfecting over the previous week.

"Stop, stop. Look, have you been practising at all this week?"

"Yes". It was the truth.

"Well, you know you really must practice more otherwise its just a waste of your time and of my time, it really is."

I squirmed uncomfortably in the chair knowing that five minutes a day really wasn't enough, and I could most definitely not pull the wool over this man's eyes.

"Look, I won't give you any more homework this week but I want you to go home and just practice 'City of New Orleans' properly over and over again, and I want to see a vast improvement next lesson, OK?"

"Yes." Hang on, was Bob taping all this? I hoped not!

By this time, Sharron had also started to take lessons with Bob. Not only did she have a much better guitar than I did (said Bob), but she had no concerns about singing or playing in front of people. I think it was about this time that Sharron and I began to practice a couple of very early Simon and Garfunkel songs and decided we'd tour the local folk club circuit. However, much to my shame, I realised quite early on that I would never be able to summon up the courage to actually get on stage and perform, despite Sharron's patient encouragement, and so I was responsible for the break-up of that short-lived, unnamed duo. Sharron, on the other hand, did go on to become quite a regular at the 'open mike' nights at the Wirral folk clubs, and she did rather well. I was often there in the audience to cheer her on as she sang the songs of Janis Ian, Al Stewart, Dan Fogelberg and other Downtown favourites. Yes, even in this aspect of our lives, we continued to 'spread the word'.

In the end, I had to admit defeat and cancelled my lessons with Bob. He had been entirely correct; towards the end I hadn't practised anywhere near enough and I was wasting my precious money. In my defence, there were too many distractions emerging - parties, boyfriends, college, concerts, pubs and clubs (I was 18, for Pete's sake!) Radio City Roadshows and 20+ page requests to write to Dave Eastwood and Johnny Jason on Downtown, and that stupid, but very much needed Saturday job along with any overtime it could provide. Actually, I did once sell Roger Blyth a pair of shoes, so it wasn't all bad! I was sad to leave my dream unfulfilled, but grateful to Bob for helping my guitar playing progress to another level. After sitting gathering dust for a number of years, the guitar was eventually sold, and so I'm ashamed to say that I no longer play in my spare time, but I do still harbour the dream to take it up once more, and this time, I know I will be more dedicated. Maybe, Bob, if you still take pupils...?

Photographs and Memories

Chris Jones reveals that one of his biggest ambitions back in the early days of Radio City was to go the Abbey Road Studios in London, so he took the opportunity of asking someone who worked for EMI whether it could be arranged. "I heard no more for ages until I got a call out of the blue one day" recalls Chris. "He had arranged a trip and could I do something else while I was there.

'What?' I asked.

'Interview Paul McCartney' he said.

Well you could have knocked me down with a feather. I quickly agreed - who wouldn't - and it was arranged. I duly headed down to London one bright day and got into a taxi at Euston and asked the cabbie to take me to Abbey Road.

'I ate goin' down there' he said. 'You can't get down the road for all the tourists havin' their photos taken on the zebra crossin'.'

When we got there he was right. In I went and was shown into Studio 2 where most of the Beatles sessions had taken place. I got a shiver down the spine as I went in - just like it does whenever I hear the Kop sing 'You'll Never Walk Alone' at Anfield. There in the middle of the studio was Paul with Denny Laine who was also a member of Wings at the time. I knew Denny of old, so the ice was broken. There was another reporter there from the NME, I think. I duly recorded my interview with Paul and he said he had something that he would like us to hear. We went up to the control room of Studio 2 where all the songs were mixed and the tape loops and sound effects were prepared for things like Sgt. Pepper. We listened to a song called 'Girls School' which Paul thought he would issue as an A side of his new single. He then played the other side - a song called 'Mull of Kintyre' complete with bagpipes. He said to me that as I was from Liverpool I could take the acetate disc (a white label) of the songs and give them an airing on City.

I got back during The Great Easton Express and Phil played 'Girls School' as an exclusive and I played 'Mull of Kintyre' as an exclusive on Downtown that night. The interview with Paul was cut and ran the next night. I still have the tape but put the acetate disc in the library. It went missing when the song was eventually released and must be worth a fortune now. Paul told me that I reminded him of Mal Evans who was the Beatles' Road Manager and fixer. That resemblance got me another interview when Paul opened his world tour at the Royal Court in Liverpool

194 Radio City

I was with the BBC by then and the interview was used all over the world and as I was working for Radio 1 at the time, it ran in their news programme, 'Newsbeat'. I remember that Norman Thomas did the interview for City and he had never met Paul before and was so nervous at meeting his hero." Norman Thomas of course remembers this interview well, and at the end of it asked Paul McCartney for his autograph. "He signed it 'all the breast', and I thought how can I show that to my mum?"

Arthur Murphy remembers those he has interviewed over the years. "One of the interviews I have always relished from my City days was the one with John Braine who wrote the best-selling novel 'Room At The Top' which was later turned into a movie. Without asking him certain questions I was able to fill in for him where he had been living when he wrote the book. I could see a scared look on his face as to how I could know so much about him until I revealed that he had written the book when he stayed with my mother-in-law in Kensington and of course he knew my wife long before I had ever met her."

Mark Jones with two members of the band Darts,
in 1978 outside the Stanley Street Studios

Arthur also recalls interviewing Henry Fonda, James Fox, John Mills, Pat Boone, Henry Cooper and Frankie Laine, who told Arthur he enjoyed listening to him on City because of his 'enthusiasm' on air. They became quite friendly and Frankie used to drive Arthur home whenever he appeared

The Heart of Liverpool

in Liverpool "I remember well one night while chatting in his car about show business, he handed me a cooked turkey leg which he hadn't had time to eat and asked me to have it; it must have been my mean and hungry look."

Guests could sometimes cause unexpected problems. In the very early days City would feature live sessions from musicians and one in particular became famous for all the wrong reasons. Mark Bolan recorded an acoustic session - just him and his guitar, and it seemed to go down very well. Unbeknownst to to the City staff, he rather cheekily swapped one of the words to his songs for a four letter word which began with 'C'. Nobody noticed at the studio, and it went out over the air. Immediately, the station began receiving phone calls from listeners who had noticed this shocking inclusion. The technicians listened back to the recording and discovered to their embarrassment that it was quite clear that he had indeed altered the word.

Mark Jones recalls embarrassing interviews as well. "Mike Harding flashing at me through the window from reception to studio one when he arrived. It was only my second interview ever on City. And I'll never forget interviewing Fleetwood Mac's Stevie Nicks, only partially clothed (her, not me) sitting on a bed in her hotel room in Manchester. She was wearing the see-through dress she wore on the cover of their album 'Rumours'. It affected me. 'Nuff said. The band were huge at the time - it was about 1978 - as the 'Rumours' album had sold by the shedload worldwide."

Screaming Lord Sutch was a regular visitor to Radio City and he and Johnny Kennedy became good friends. "He was often on my show" says Johnny "and was always good for a laugh, And afterwards we'd pop round to the Post House in Cumberland Street for a few pints.

"Dave Sutch had started in the 60s with his own band, and took a coffin on stage and sang such classics as 'Dracula's Daughter' and 'Jack the Ripper'. He also had his own radio station called Radio Sutch, on which he just played his own records.

"He came on my show when he was fighting the election as chairman of The Monster Raving Loony Party, and we hit it off right from the start. He was always ready to have a laugh and he didn't seem to take himself too seriously. And not all his ideas were potty; he was the first one to campaign for the voting age to be lowered to 18, and he thought dog licences should be abolished.

"He was very impressed when Radio City sent me to do broadcasts in places like Australia, New Zealand, Singapore and New York, and on one of his visits to the station he asked me to accept the position of Foreign

194 Radio City

Minister in The Monster Raving Loony Party. I accepted the post like a shot, and a few weeks later we had a celebration party on air. And as I have never been sacked I presume I still hold the position. If it hadn't been for Radio City I'd never have met him."

Joe Butler recalls that working at Radio City allowed him the privilege of meeting and interviewing plenty of country music stars. "Another hero of

Johnny Kennedy and Cliff Richard at Radio City, 1980s

mine though who I got to meet was Hank Marvin of The Shadows. He had come to do an interview in one of the other shows and was waiting to go into the studio. We got chatting and it turned out that he too has a great love of country music but didn't get much chance to play any. He was a real nice guy and very humble considering his status in the music business."

Johnny Jason and The Great ELO Debate

Johnny Jason in Amsterdam 2004, at the Radio Caroline Reunion

In 1979 one of my favourite bands, The Electric Light Orchestra, released a new album called 'Discovery'. Of course, as self-proclaimed number one fan, I went straight out and bought it, but immediately felt something was awry. With the possible exception of 'Don't Bring Me Down', it was extremely tacky. My favourite member of the band, the violinist, and current love of my life (well, one of them anyway) Mik Kaminski wasn't even credited. Neither were the cellists, Melvyn Gale and Hugh McDowell. There were strings on the album, but very much in the background. Bev Bevan's mighty drums also appeared to be muted, as if he was playing in another room. The songs were weak with - oh horror - more than a pinch of disco, horrible tinny keyboards and a liberal sprinkling of naff vocal effects. To cap it all Jeff Lynne, never one of pop's most eloquent lyricists I have to admit, surpassed himself this time with his nonsensical lines. Anyway, you'll get the gist.

194 Radio City

ELO had evolved with each album. Both line-up and style had developed and changed, sometimes quite dramatically over the years. This was a good thing. But Discovery, or rather 'Disco Very' as it was mockingly called at the time, was too much change to handle. 'Last Train to London', with its disco beat and mirror ball feel, was the worst offender on a truly shoddy album. I felt I had been cheated. I'm sorry that this isn't a balanced criticism, but if you really haven't guessed by now, I loathed it.

A bit of a joke nowadays, it should be remembered that ELO were big then, and I mean really big. The albums 'New World Record' and 'Out of the Blue' were classics, staying in the charts for years at a time. But what did other long-standing ELO fans think of the latest offering, I wondered?

Johnny Jason was to be the DJ on whose Wednesday night Downtown shows I would vent my anger. Johnny (real name: Rudigar Jonathan von Etzdorf, but better known to his fans as JJ) had started out in radio in 1971 when he was in Australia. In 1973, he returned to Britain and auditioned, but failed to get a job with Capital Radio. He then ended up on the relaunched Radio Caroline for the next couple of years, and following that he worked at Metro Radio in Newcastle and Radio Orwell in Ipswich. Whilst here, JJ felt the lure of Radio Caroline once again and returned for a short time - not a man to stay anywhere for very long, clearly! Despite all this moving around, he built up a loyal fan base, and regularly appeared in nationally held Top Ten DJ lists. In 1978 he joined Radio City, where he says was asked to cover the 10 till 2 slot on Downtown. "And" he says "I remained here for four very happy years. As far as the music goes, it was mostly mellow soul, people like Marvin Gaye, The Emotions, Michael Jackson, Minnie Ripperton, Heatwave, Earth, Wind & Fire, etc."

Bearing in mind the above, it may seem surprising that I chose Johnny's weekday Downtown rather than Dave Eastwood's weekend show. Dave Eastwood was an ELO fan like myself, often having their singles as his Record of the Week, and would have been the obvious choice, however JJ it was. Some other listeners had already started a debate about the band's declining standards and I felt compelled to join in. One of these listeners was 18 year old Tony Hardaker from Bootle. He certainly seemed to feel the same way as I did as he seethed about the dire 'Diary of Horace Wimp'.

Tony recalls "When I was studying for exams, and after I left school in 1978, I started listening to Radio City, usually late evening, and through the night until about 3 am. I enjoyed the light-hearted banter from the DJs, the odd (ie strange) requests from fellow insomniacs and jobless. The DJs themselves meant nothing to me until I heard DJ Johnny Jason read out a

78

The Heart of Liverpool

request for an early ELO track and a comment from the requester about the latest LP, Discovery, being poor compared to the two previous LPs. I started writing in to complain about falling ELO standards when they released a track called 'The Diary of Horace Wimp', which I'd previously thought would only be an album filler."

Johnny Jason tried to be diplomatic. If I moaned about 'Last Train', or Tony about 'Horace Wimp', he'd say in true JJ speak that it had been a "gigantic smash" and therefore a large proportion of the record buying public must disagree with us. To his credit, he would always allow us to try to prove our point in music by playing our requests for '10538 Overture', 'Dreaming of 4000', or 'Fire on High'. And indeed for weeks afterwards people came up to me in school saying they'd heard the songs and agreed with my point of view. They hadn't realised the older ELO stuff was so good. I finally felt vindicated.

Very soon, a weary JJ tried unsuccessfully to put an end to this ongoing debate by giving out Tony's address on air and inviting us all to write to him so we could carry on our discussion together. A lot of us did, myself included, but for a while, spurred on by our common bond, we continued to bombard JJ with yet more letters proclaiming that ELO owed us more than this paltry rubbish, and all mentioning each other as proof, we felt, of popular feeling! Believe me, hell hath no fury like an ELO fan scorned.

Tony Hardaker, who now lives in Edinburgh, recalls that around this time he was invited to a meeting of the rather grandly named Liverpool branch of the ELO Appreciation Society. It turned out that the 'meetings' were held in the front room of a house in Childwall, and were attended by a bloke and his girlfriend plus a couple of their mates, and Tony and that was it. The meeting consisted of sitting around playing the older, finer ELO albums and drinking cups of tea. Tony stayed as long as was polite before making his exit, and he never attended another 'meeting', although he continued to carry the flag for his favourite band over the air as before, not to mention trying to blag a lift to ELO's Wembley concert in one of his requests - in this he was unsuccessful.

Another ELO fan who regularly wrote in to JJ's show was Paul Leckie. Still a couple of years away from working at the station himself, he was still a Radio City listener, and a fan of JJ's style. "What a fantastic voice! All my friends at school listened to him and I regularly wrote in as the ELO Fanatic as I was crazy about the group. I seemed to get a mention every week and JJ played my favourite tracks." Paul also remembers how JJ would have a featured album of the week and how he would always write in to request one of ELO's albums.

194 Radio City

OK so history has proven that ELO, or rather Jeff Lynne as it was all his fault, didn't heed our warnings that it would only end in disaster and he went on, unbelievably, to make even worse ELO albums such as 'Secret Messages' and 'Time'. Sadly for me, I was never to buy another record by my beloved Electric Light Orchestra. Eventually the band imploded and the Travelling Wilburys and ELO Part 2 mutated forth from the remains...I rest my case!

JJ, however, did remain during his time at City one of my favourite DJs. Like Paul, I ended up with a regular request slot (between 11 and midnight on a Wednesday) when the poor man would have to read out the name of practically every girl in Oxley Senior Comprehensive School's Lower VIth, not to mention what seems like at least 50 other friends and dubious acquaintances.

One of the reasons I found JJ so fascinating was that he would come out with the most wonderful phrases to describe a record. My absolute favourite was "Disco Bop Galore". Unfortunately, I cannot for the life of me remember to which track he was referring, but it was marvellous 'JJ speak' just the same. In fact "galore" cropped up quite a lot, as did "swirling strings and heavenly choirs" (usually ELO) and "jingling jangling guitars" (with the stress on the first syllable of guitars), "pulsating bass" and "bringing us in in rip-roaring style". DJs just don't do it like that anymore, do they? Actually, they'd probably become a laughing stock overnight if they tried, but back then, well, it was just JJ's style, wasn't it? Real '70s DJs, how we loved them. Ironic though that John Jason, as he now prefers to be known, ex-pirate and long-haired, heavy rock loving hippie, now has one of the most conservative jobs of all: reading the news for the BBC World Service!

Jingle Jangle

Of course, I wasn't the only one to be this fanatical about Radio City - not at all. Some people were so hugely affected by the magnificence of what came over the airwaves that it affected their life and choice of career. Nick Parton is now working as a DJ at Radio Maldwyn in mid-Wales, and as a young boy growing up in St Asaph, North Wales, he was fairly obsessed with Radio City too. I asked him about his memories and was astounded at how much detail he still recalls.

"I'd always listened to City since I can remember as my mum used to have the radio on in the kitchen. My very first memory of City was of Norman Thomas. My mum was a huge fan of his and I was always being told to 'shush' when he spoke! Norman presented breakfast and later a Sunday morning show called 'Heads and Tails', originally presented by Billy Butler and Wally Scott.

DJ line-up from 1987: Brian Ford, Johnny Kennedy, Kevin Keatings, Mark Jones, Jeff Cooper, Paul Jordan and Norman Thomas

"I started to become interested in Radio City and radio as a media in 1981 when my mum and dad bought me a radio cassette recorder for my birthday. During my childhood, my heroes were the likes of Norman

194 Radio City

Thomas, who remains my hero to this day, Phil Easton, Mark Jones, Dave Eastwood, Billy Butler and Kevin Keatings to name but a few. Where other kids admired people such as Spandau Ballet, Duran Duran and Madonna, my heroes and icons were Radio City Djs!

"I would always go to bed with my transistor radio and listen to City before falling asleep. I always listened to Kevin Keatings on Downtown with his featured artist and constant interruptions from Roland Rat! He always took the mickey out of of Nicky Brown, calling him "Nappy Brown" because he was so young. Kevin was very clued up on music and presented the show with enormous enthusiasm. The Peaceful Hour must hold some of my favourite memories from those days. Great smooth music under the duvet! I remember Paul Leckie presenting weekend Downtown, who is a very underrated presenter. And I also recall Paul Jordan doing weekend Downtown with his 'steamy letters' spot and his constant rib-taking of Johnny Kennedy's record 'Stay in your Own Back Yard'.

Sarah Smithard, now Managing Director of the Marcher Group of radio stations run by GCap, who are of course, rivals to City and Emap, admits that although she didn't have ambitions to be a DJ, Radio City certainly fostered within her a huge love of music which remains to this day, and which she can definitely state has led to her being involved within the music media.

There are two Radio City websites dedicated to the early days of the station, both very different in style and both run by big Radio City fans. I was interested to find out what they felt was so good about City in the early years that made them devote so much time to creating their own personal shrines.

Nigel Bateman is not only a fan, but he also used to work at Radio City as a producer and engineer. "I started the website because there wasn't one out there at the time" he explained. "It was going to be a jingle site originally but after getting together with Carl Dears, who was a friend and another big Radio City fan, there was a lot more that I could add. Carl was a great help because of his knowledge and memory and also because he had lots of pictures and audio that I didn't have. The site works because I've been not only a listener but also a staff member. I can see things from two camps. That's also helped me to make contacts to include in the site.

"I've made some good friends with the website and we've been able to have our own little 194 get-togethers. Its just a bit of fun. I hate the term 'anorak'. I used to keep quiet about my keen interest when I worked at City because I didn't want them calling me 'anorak', although now I think I

The Heart of Liverpool

should have made people take more notice; I might have collected a lot more than I have today. Who knows?"

Nigel also has his own personal memories of his time at Stanley Street. DJ Phil Sayer was a good friend, and Nigel recalls one particular episode when a little on-air joke was not shared by the powers that be.

"We had the new station jingle package that had just been introduced and everyone was talking about it. I was in the studio and happened to mention to Phil that one of the jingles sounded as though the singers were singing "Shut up! Your favourite music is here: Radio City Gold." (They were actually singing a sort of "show-wop edoo de oh" kind of thing at the start.) So Phil decides to tell the story on air as though his slightly deaf old mother had just called to ask why the jingle singers were telling people to shut up, because your favourite music is here. I was in pleats of laughter in the studio, trying to stifle my giggles as Phil is trying to explain to his mother that wasn't what they were singing. He played the jingle and tried to explain it all in his very dry style. But as soon as he played the next song, Richard Duncan, Programme Controller, came bursting into the studio, all red-faced and spitting feathers. 'They're *not* singing "Shut up!" It's not that at all. We've paid thousands of pounds for this jingle package! How could your mother think they were singing *that*?' "

You may think it was only a jingle and what was all the fuss about, but jingles are a very serious business to some people. Brian Jones hosts a Radio City tribute site which is primarily jingle based, but also includes some recent interviews with ex-Radio City people.

"It wasn't until 1976 that I started listening to City, then I thought to myself why don't I buy a cassette recorder and record the jingles for posterity?" Brian explains. "This would then unknowingly turn into a ten year crusade of recording one heck of a lot of output from City's Stanley Street Studios. To this end I eventually recorded 244 cassettes and 15 reels of material. These jingles would include the packages from 1974, 1977, 1979 and 1982/3."

So, I wondered, what was it about jingles that warranted so much devotion and tape space? "In 1976 I became short term unemployed" said Brian "so had plenty of time on my hands, plus also a new tape recorder, so it went from there. My discovery of jingles came about because of the fact that jingles are like very short songs. The difference between a jingle and a fully fledged song is that the jingle has to tell you what its about in a very short space of time, ie 10 seconds. Its got to grab you straightaway. I think I was a bit bored with some of the songs that were being played on the radio and the jingles sounded better."

194 Radio City

Following the completion of Brian's City jingle collecting in the early to mid 1980s, they were put away for over a decade.

"For the next 12 years the tapes would sit in their boxes gathering dust. That was until 1998 when I built my own computer after seeing computer software at Shore FM where I was Commercial Production Manager. This computer software could manipulate audio and you could literally do anything with the click of a mouse. You could produce sound effects which if you were to do it on reel to reel, could take minutes, but with the computer it was seconds. I thought to myself, what about those tapes of Radio City jingles? I could put them onto CD. I then started to transfer my jingles into the digital domain.

"It was also at this time I came up with the idea of letting people listen to my jingles and see my memorabilia of Radio City which I have collected over the years - and there was a lot of material. The internet was the answer, so I started to create The Brian Jones Radio City Tribute Website, which has turned into a labour of love. Since I've started working on my City stuff again, the enthusiasm has returned to the days of the '70s and '80s."

Dave Eastwood - A Musical Mentor

The author with Dave Eastwood at the Bebington Show 1979

So what had led to this desire that I should put pen to paper and celebrate 194 Radio City and the music it played? And why now, suddenly, all these years later? I can put it down to one particular DJ from the 1970s.

Dave Eastwood was the Radio City DJ who was the biggest influence on my maturing musical taste. He certainly wasn't the first DJ who introduced me to Harry Chapin (that was Roger Blyth) or even Chris de Burgh (that was Chris Jones), but it was he who nurtured that initial spark of interest in their music, along with that of many others, fed it and helped it to grow. He had an infectious enthusiasm for the music he played, and a very individual, intimate style that made you feel as though you were at a friend's house listening to their favourite records, not just to a faceless radio DJ. I have so much to thank him for. Artists who would have been ignored in the main, maybe because they were generally seen, by myself as well as others, as middle-of-the-road or maybe belonging to another generation, now sit alongside the more readily accepted greats often because of just one track

194 Radio City

on an otherwise average album. Sometimes that track would be so incredibly magnificent to me that embarrassment would go out of the window. A perfect example of this is hidden within the Johnny Mathis album 'I Only Have Eyes For You'. The album is complete and utter dross, with the exception of one track, 'Yellow Roses On Her Gown', which had me searching for this long-deleted LP for many years in mounting desperation. Unfortunately, I have been unable to discover anything about the person who wrote it, but it sounds like a lost Jimmy Webb classic. This song has never received the recognition it deserves, at least in this country, but why is that? The song is achingly beautiful and I wish more people knew of its existence, because its difficult for me to convince people to even give it a try when they have their own understandably preconceived ideas of Mr Mathis. Dave, however, was able to convince us.

Being a Radio City DJ in the 1970s, before the playlist became god, was the perfect way to reveal these little gems to listeners, especially those who were too lazy to turn off the radio when they were listening in their beds to that wonderful long-lost City goldmine that was The Peaceful Hour. And for me there were to be many discoveries: 'Jonathan Livingstone Seagull' that emotive soundtrack album by Neil Diamond; Colin Blunstone's 'Ennismore'; Clifford T Ward's 'Mantle Pieces'; 'Between the Lines' by Janice Ian; the back catalogue of Scott Walker, Randy Newman, Harry Nilsson. There was an instant connection between DJ and listener there too which I enjoyed. Quite often Dave would play a record and I would be sitting there as it drew to a close with tears streaming down my face at the sheer beauty of it and then Dave would say something along the lines of "Beautiful record..... Oh I do love a good cry, don't you?" and there we'd be laughing together - I felt there was definitely a musical bond there, that few others would understand. It was so special to me back then, and there was never any chance of my falling asleep during The Peaceful Hour, or any hour of Dave's show, that was for sure.

When Dave Eastwood joined Radio City in the mid '70s, it was as a freelance DJ and this meant he was free to produce advertisements and do voice-overs and in both of these he is remembered as being highly skilled. During his time at City, he tended to fill in for other more regular presenters. He also became the resident DJ at Leighton Court Country Club in Neston. For the most part, he fitted in well at the station, and became a much-loved member of City's staff. This much is straightforward, but his background was a little more unusual.

Long-time friend and fellow DJ, David Hamilton, who is now at Saga Radio in the West Midlands, had known Dave since they were both 17 years

The Heart of Liverpool

of age when they first met during their National Service and were posted to the RAF base at Compton Bassett in Wiltshire. David remembers it well. "Neither of us had experience of DJ work at this point, but we put ourselves forward and were accepted. We were to broadcast over the camp in what was known as CFN - the Compton Forces Network."

Following this spell, it is common knowledge that 'Diddy' David moved on to Radio 1 and eventually become a celebrity DJ nationally, but what was Dave's next move? Well, believe it or not, he became a Methodist Lay Preacher. After a brief period working as a car mechanic, he had begun working with teenagers at the Birkenhead YMCA and it was there that he became a popular local DJ, picking up the nickname 'Dave the Rave'. It was also at one of these events that he first set eyes on Tricia, the girl who was to become his wife. It was love at first sight on Dave's part, although Tricia was allegedly a little sceptical at first saying she didn't really fancy having a methodist minister as a boyfriend!

Because of his religious background and also his interest in pop music, Dave naturally took an interest in the Christian bands that were around Merseyside at the time, and for a while managed one of them, The Witnesses.

Eddie Boyes is someone who remembers those days, being a member of the Christian band Crossbeats with whom Dave worked during the Rally For Youth movement in the late 1960s. "I do remember Dave being a very lively and dynamic youth worker who was very involved in 'Youth for Christ' in Liverpool, and a good youth speaker and evangelist in his own right. I can see him now bounding on the stage - dark suit, tight trousers with a very bubbly personality. He had a strong Christian faith, though I am not sure how this developed when we lost touch with him in the '70s. He was extremely helpful to us in the early days, especially with transport, but in other ways too."

David Hamilton gradually lost touch with Dave Eastwood after their days at CFN, but when David started a job as a television announcer at Didsbury in Manchester, quite suddenly out of the blue he was contacted by Dave again and their friendship was rekindled. "He was quite square then" laughed David, "if you told a dirty joke he would be disgusted, although he was still very good company, and it was at this time he expressed an interest in radio to me again. I mentioned him to John Wilcox, who was in charge of Radio 1 in those days, and he took Dave on, initially to be an interviewer at their station in Manchester."

Along with Radio 1, Dave would work at BBC Radio Manchester, Radio Teeside (later Radio Cleveland) and eventually hosted the mid-morning

194 Radio City

show on Manchester's brand new independent station, Piccadilly Radio. It was from here that he made the move to Liverpool and Radio City.

One of Dave's first regular shows on joining Radio City was the children's programme 'Ring-a-Ding' which he presented with the help of his son Richard. Richard, now a top Liverpool-based architect who has designed, amongst other things, the interiors of The Pan-American Club and Baby Cream at the Albert Dock, was the only child to regularly help present a show on Radio City. He had been a child model when very young, as well as providing the voice-over for advertisements featuring a child cartoon-type character. From there it was easy enough to slip into radio broadcasting alongside his Dad. "I think I must have been about 10 years old at the time." recalls Richard.

'Ring-a-Ding' ran every Sunday morning for about two years. It specifically targeted the under-12s with requests, birthday mentions, dedications, competitions and the Radio City Children's Club. The programme went out completely live but amazingly, despite this, Richard doesn't remember any major catastrophes, and does remember rather enjoying himself, along with the notoriety that came with it. "People at school did know about the show and who my Dad was and stuff and, yes, I suppose I did become something of a minor celebrity there, although I was never bullied because of it. I didn't really know any different though. I was able to go to concerts from quite an early age so I was lucky in that respect. I can remember going to see Neil Sedaka and Neil Diamond, people like that." Richard readily admits though that he didn't share his Dad's musical taste, much preferring the progressive rock genre. But it was thanks to his Dad that he was also able to meet a lot of celebrities at the Stanley Street Studios. "I can remember walking in there and seeing Robert Plant, that was good. And sitting in on interviews Dad did with people like Cliff Richard. I really enjoyed that. I can also remember being in reception and seeing Keith Chegwin and hearing him swear. I was so shocked. Keith Chegwin was the first person I'd ever heard swear!" Ironically, 'Ring-a-Ding' was to finish its run when it was was replaced by a show hosted by Keith Chegwin, with the rather uninspired title of 'Its Cheggers'.

Speaking for myself, Dave first came to my attention when he covered Downtown briefly following Arthur Murphy's shock exit. Having been a big Arthur Murphy fan, I was more than a little upset to hear this new voice suddenly taking over my favourite show, however I was soon to be won over.

Dave Eastwood eventually took over the weekend Downtown slot full time and settled into it as comfortably as though he'd always been there, and

The Heart of Liverpool

Sharron and I became mad 'Eastie Beastie' fans and pretty soon two of his most regular correspondents. Music by this time was becoming all-important to us and Dave was only too happy to introduce us to a wonderful new world inhabited in the main by singer-songwriters such Clifford T Ward, Paul Simon, Christopher Rainbow, David Gates and so many more. Backing musicians and musical arrangers would regularly receive reverential mentions too, in fact it is no coincidence that Richard Hewson became such a favourite arranger of mine during this time. Sharron and I learned so much about what and who made our favourite records so special.

Our requests to the show were self-indulgent, I'll be honest. Reams and reams of record requests and general chit-chat. And Dave, who dispensed with the Radio City record library quite early on, preferring to bring his own records in, was more than happy to play the music he loved. It must have been a wonderful feeling to know that he had managed to pass that love over to a new, younger audience.

He had a voice that was made for radio, and many people to whom I have spoken in the course of researching this book say exactly the same thing when I mention Dave. People like David Hamiton who says "Its unfortunate he came to radio quite late, in his late 20s. If he had gone straight from the RAF into radio, he would have been much, much bigger than he was - his was a real talent and he had a natural, overwhelming enthusiasm for music." What he definitely was not was the most organised or slick DJ in the world. But he was down to earth and could make us laugh as much as the songs he played could make us cry. As the years passed, we grew to know Dave as a friend as well, and we found the man outside the studio was, much to our delight, exactly the same as the man behind the mike. On our Saturday mornings outside the studios, as well as at the Roadshows, Dave was the person we saw most often and got to know the best.

As Sharron and I grew older, we began to go regularly to concerts, usually at the Empire or newly reopened Royal Court. The music we listened to over the radio and on record was no longer enough in itself. We wanted to see our heroes in the flesh and experience live music. We did the usual stuff; bought programmes and t shirts, and met the stars themselves after the show and had our photographs taken with them. We would often be spotted by Dave outside the theatres afterwards or in the lobby during the interval. He would come scurrying over, as was his usual manner and ask us what we thought of the show and we would chat about music and whatever else was currently going on in our lives. Of course the record requests continued every weekend, and we were still travelling to the roadshows. Life was pretty great.

One of our most enduring memories of Dave was one time he had been chatting to Sharron and myself during one of our Saturday mornings outside the Stanley Street Studios. After five minutes or so, he suddenly said "Do you fancy a cup of tea?" Of course we agreed and off we all went to the Armadillo Tea Rooms round the corner in Mathew Street. Dave who always walked quickly, dashed ahead while Sharron and I followed behind at a more sedate pace, looking at each other with a strange mixture of pride and disbelief. Once there we shared a pot of Earl Grey along with some cake, and merrily discussed music and Radio City gossip for a further half an hour. Bliss! It was always wonderful to spend time with Dave because he was as zealous about music as we were, and as two teenage girls whose tastes were at odds with most of our friends, we finally had someone else with whom we could share our fabulous obsession, and the fact that we were the same age as his own children meant he was perfectly at ease chatting to us.

Sharron left school in 1979, a year before I did. I had decided to stay on in the Sixth Form and take some A levels while deciding what to do with my life. It was around this time that my requests to Radio City spilled over into the weekday Downtown shows as well. Nearly every Wednesday night during term time, Johnny Jason would play a request for me between 11 and midnight. And as with Dave, I would sometimes get a mention from JJ anyway, even if I didn't have time to write in. I still have the letters and Christmas cards I received from both Dave Eastwood and JJ dating from that time, keeping me informed as to what they were up to. I kept in touch with both for a while when they moved away from Radio City and from Liverpool. I took English and Art at A level, and toyed with the ideas of either journalism or Art School. But eventually, a little over half way through my studies, I realised Sixth Form was no improvement on the previous dreary three years at my school. I felt stifled, and I enrolled instead at a local college where I studied something completely different. Over the next year or so, gradually and without ceremony, the request writing came to an end.

The Heart of Liverpool

I last heard from Dave out of the blue in a letter dated November 1983:

Hi Kath

How are you? I thought you might like to know that I'm going to be on 208 Radio Luxembourg during March. I don't know which show I'll be doing yet, but it should be easy to find out. If you do tune in (hopefully!) can you let me know c/o Radio Luxembourg, Hertford Street, London West 1? Its only temporary at the moment and I'll be back on City in April but hopefully I'll be in for a job, if all goes well, later in the year.

love and cuddles

Dave

However life moves on and despite tuning in to Radio Luxembourg on one occasion to hear Dave again, that part of my life was effectively over. It wasn't until many years later that I began to wonder what had happened to the 'Eastie Beastie' and mentioned it in passing to Sharron, saying that I would have to search the internet for details of what he was doing now, maybe with a view to getting in touch. Sharron agreed and said she would do the same. Months passed, but except for the odd perfunctory check via an internet search engine, I'll admit I hadn't spent too much time looking. After all, I now had two young children keeping me busy day and night and there would be plenty of time in the future, wouldn't there?

But by now it was 2002 and I had already left it too late. Much too late. Sharron phoned one Saturday evening with the mind-numbing news that Dave was dead. She had found a simple line hidden within a Radio Luxembourg fan site:

Dave Eastwood + died 19** (leukaemia)

Of course, she said, it may not be true, as it was clearly vague and only a fan site. I felt sick and made a decision to contact the site immediately to find out the truth. When I hadn't heard back from the Radio Luxembourg fan site by the end of the week, I really couldn't bear the uncertainty any longer. I could think of nothing else. At this stage I was at a loss to explain why the news hit me so hard. After all I hadn't really thought about Dave, except in passing, for years. My thoughts drifted back to those damp

194 Radio City

Saturday mornings camped outside the Radio City Studios and I tried to remember which DJs would be the ones most likely to remember Dave. Mark Jones was certainly around at the same time and I decided to give him a try, although I did not know how close he had been to Dave. As well as DJing he now also runs his own company so I emailed him there and received a reply which confirmed that Dave had indeed died of leukaemia. He had been diagnosed in approximately August 1988 and had died in the following March. Mark said that Dave had last worked on Essex Radio and suggested I contact them. Unprepared for what might follow, I sent off an email the very next day.

It wasn't long before I received a reply from Pete Sipple, who ran the Essex Radio website for former employees of the station. He remembered Dave Eastwood fondly, having worked alongside him during the late 1980s and told me he had remained in touch with a few people who would have worked with him around that time. He passed my request for information on to them and I was amazed, and deeply touched by the steady flow of memories that came through my computer over the next few weeks. The intervening years were finally pieced together and though at times deeply distressing, the overall effect was nevertheless heart-warming. All who knew him clearly loved him, and my faith in this man's uniqueness was justified.

I learned that Dave began working at Essex Radio in 1985. He had taken over the afternoon drive time show and had started to host quiz games over the air. A regular feature on Radio City for a number of years, this was a relatively new idea to Essex Radio and one which quickly found favour with the listeners who warmed to Dave's bubbly personality. It made me smile to read that staff who worked with him recall that he was a great presenter being both natural and charismatic, but one with absolutely no organisational skills whatsoever - often being in a muddle on the air. No improvements there then!

However this trait of Dave's, which had been so much a part of the man throughout his whole broadcasting career, was eventually to take on a poignant twist. A former Managing Director at Essex Radio recalled how Dave's cancer first became apparent. Apparently, one of the programme controllers had come to him expressing concern that Dave's on-air performance was slipping. On listening in to a couple of shows for himself, and speaking to colleagues of Dave's, it was clear that there was a problem, as Dave was sounding much too blasé, cutting the beginnings and endings of songs and botching the commercials on a increasingly frequent basis. A meeting was swiftly arranged and Dave was given a warning that if

The Heart of Liverpool

improvements were not forthcoming, the station would have to let him go. It was only now that Dave admitted to having felt unwell and exhausted for some time. Between themselves, it was agreed that he should visit his GP as soon as possible.

Returning from this appointment, Dave said he had been given a physical and would be going for some routine blood tests. He continued on air. Then one day, during a live broadcast, Dave received a call from his GP saying that the results of his tests were back and they were not good. He was asked to return urgently. Despite this ominous news, Dave continued his programme as if nothing had happened.

His GP informed him that he had a rare type of leukaemia which usually struck young children and did have a very high success rate in that group. However, it was also a type which proved particularly virulent in older people and the prognosis was not good. Chemotherapy was the only option.

From the outset, Dave was determined to continue broadcasting for as long as possible. It was what he loved and what he did best. After much discussion, the Board of Directors allowed the station to manage the programme in their own fashion. Dave was to continue on the air but would be given someone to assist him on the technical side. He continued with his predominantly music based programme, which was now interspersed with a daily commentary of what he was doing, how he was feeling, the treatment he was having, the people who were treating him and the drugs he was using. He wanted to lessen people's fear of cancers and their treatments and by using his unique position, hopefully do some good and raise awareness, and maybe some money for research into a cure. The show immediately proved popular and successful, and it was all carried out in a professional and upbeat way.

Eventually it became clear that Dave was too ill to leave hospital, but he managed to persuade doctors to allow him to record interviews for on-air broadcast from within the hospital ward. During this time, the Dave Eastwood Leukaemia Appeal was launched, and the people of Essex, who had grown to love and respect this man, rallied round and gave generously.

Tragically, Dave did not respond well to the chemotherapy and was eventually left blind and immobile. Despite this, he remained optimistic and even expressed concern to his colleagues that a job would be there for him at Essex Radio when he recovered. He was always assured that it would, despite the fact that it was clear to everyone else that he was dying. The end came quietly, with his family at his bedside. He was buried at St Lawrence's Church, Eastwood, near Southend Airport. A cheque was presented to the hospital for a prodigious £75,000 - the proceeds of the Dave Eastwood Leukaemia Fund. This was matched by the NHS and used to open a new ward at the Whitechapel Hospital for the treatment of patients with leukaemia.

One of the most liberating aspects of growing older is the fact that I can finally admit to my disparate musical legacy. It no longer matters whether something is fashionable, or accepted by others as good music. I'd always liked this stuff, I just hadn't been able to admit to it for so long. Suddenly, just as I did when I discovered all the wonderful singer-songwriters and musicians for the very first time through Radio City, I want to share these precious finds with everyone again. I am finally in a position to buy all those albums I couldn't afford in my teens. As people are discarding their '70s vinyl for peanuts, I am thoroughly enjoying myself snapping them up. And if I hadn't discovered Dave's death and realised with a shock what great joy he had brought me, I wouldn't now be bawling my eyes out over Janis Ian's wonderfully poignant 'Tea and Sympathy' - it gets me every time - I possibly never would have gone further than 'At 17'. Nor would I be sitting in The Pacific Road Arts Centre watching Dean Friedman sing the beautiful 'Shopping Bag Ladies' just a few feet away from me. And even with newer musicians, I really feel as though somewhere I still have some help, some guidance from Dave. Sure I miss the banter, the silly requests and chats about music over tea or wherever. But as a mentor, corny as it may sound, he is still there, very much a part of my musical self, evangelically egging me on when I'm unsure about an album or whether to go to a concert by some old 'has-been'. Even if I wanted to, I know I couldn't disentangle him. And I realise now that's why his death had been such a huge blow, but also an awakening. It really wasn't difficult to understand. So much of what I listen to within a song has been tutored by Dave. I automatically listen out for specific chord changes, clever little tricks that songwriters use to tug on the heartstrings. I would without a doubt have always loved music, and quite possibly would have reached these discoveries on my own, but I like to believe that Dave made a difference. And that is something for which I will be eternally grateful.

The Heart of Liverpool

The Radio City Retro Fest 2004

Empty places echoing past.
All I have to do is close my eyes
I can't tell which is now and which was then.
Give me what I cry for, what I would have gladly died for,
Take me to the young years that I loved.
I've made the last correction
And my path has changed direction
I'm thinkin' like I did when I was young.

Chris Rainbow 'Give Me What I Cry For'

So here we were at last, 15th May 2004, and Sharron and I were embarking on our evening of pure, unashamed nostalgia - the Radio City Retro Fest. Our men had been dispatched to the pub and the wine was flowing, as were the memories.

Along with boxes full of cassettes and loads of vinyl - LPs and singles - I would also be able to reveal the two websites dedicated to the early days of Radio City. They contained photographs of the DJs, all the old jingles, personal memories and details of what some of the older DJs are doing now. As Sharron didn't possess a computer, I was pretty certain she wouldn't know about them, especially as they were fairly new sites.

I'd stored the best jingles to play back, which I started to do now. It was strange. Although Sharron and I had spent most of our teenage years living for and with Radio City, and talking about little else, we had rarely listened to the station in the same room together. Now we could listen to those jingles and even the old adverts, laugh about the ones we remember, and hear each other's requests side by side. They were happy memories, but there was still an undercurrent of sadness there at that which was now so clearly gone forever.

I had advised Sharron to bring any old Radio City memorabilia she still had and I was amazed and not a little envious, to see she still had the old DJ poster. There they all were: Mark Joenz, Dave Eastwood, Roger Blyth,

194 Radio City

Dave Lincoln etc - all the '70s DJs looking resplendent in their 194 jumpers, eye-catching shirts and strange hairdos. God only knows where my copy went, I mean, I would never have thrown it away... would I? The wine was obviously working its magic as giggling, we located a piece of tired old blue tac and stuck it up on the wall like some tatty, faded religious relic.

The drink continued to go down well - too well - as we pored over albums we'd forgotten, and some which we'd never admit to liking, never mind owning at other times or in other places: "Oh, Steely Dan, I didn't know you had this! I LOVED them!" and even "Leo Sayer had some really great songs, didn't he?" and remembering when certain people used to have integrity: "Wasn't Chris de Burgh WONDERFUL back then? 'At The End of a Perfect Day' - I still listen to that sometimes, and 'Satin Green Shutters' .... God, what went wrong?" and getting tearful over those who had died: John Lennon, Clifford T Ward, Harry Chapin, Jim Croce, Harry Nilsson ... not to mention Roger Blyth and, of course, Dave Eastwood. So many wonderful people are now lost to us.

Sharron suggested we play some old requests and I opened the ancient cassette boxes and we were propelled willingly inside that musical time machine back to our favourite show, Downtown. The requests are amusing with names of people long forgotten. Requests to cheer us up as we sit our exams, requests for those leaving for University, and ultimately those first embarrassing dedications for boyfriends. They were clearly from a time of innocence and life on the verge of something... A metamorphosis was occurring again, as in the early listening years, only from our present vantage point it is clear we were leaving something very special behind. It was time to return, if only for a while.

So not long after our drunken Retro Fest, on 21st October 2004 Radio City celebrated 30 amazing years on air. Sadly, the Stanley Street Studios and most of the original people have long gone, but thankfully not all of them. When you visit Liverpool city centre now, if you look up into the sky you will have no difficulty in seeing City's new home. High above everything is the St John's Beacon, the old Tower Restaurant, with 'Radio City 96.7' clearly visible for miles around - still proclaiming confidently that City are miles above the competition. And Radio City is, in fact, still the biggest commercial radio station outside London.

The Heart of Liverpool

All that remains for me to say, Radio City, is I hope I'm around to see you celebrate another 30 years at least. From the dream of a Merseyside journalist to this. You have come a long, long way. And yes, you have changed, but then haven't we all? Long may your voice continue to be heard. Radio City, the true Heart of Liverpool. I'll drink to that!

194 Radio City

Dave Lincoln returns triumphant to Stanley Street as Head of Music in 1986

POSTSCRIPT
1984 and beyond - time for a change?

By 1981, Radio City was just about at the top of the tree and was the envy of all other independent local radio stations. Its weekly audience reach was almost fifty percent. By this time, DJs such as Mark Jones, Norman Thomas, Phil Easton, Billy Butler and Johnny Kennedy were part of a consistent line-up of presenters who had their own brand of humour and personality, something frowned upon today, but which back then, meant the station had a loyal following. The award nominations were coming in thick and fast, for the news department who by this time had a team of 15 journalists, as well as for the music and talk shows, and the station's reputation seemed sealed. In Merseyside we were proud of our station and barely a car was seen around the area which did not proudly display at least one 194 logo car sticker. It was a brand to us as strong as Coca Cola, which ironically would often been seen linked with Radio City a few years later as the sponsorship deal took place.

By now, many of the original DJs, reporters and newsreaders were moving on to bigger things. Elton Welsby and Clive Tyldesley, City's sports reporters, both made their mark on ITV football commentating. Roger Blyth presented Granada Reports on TV, and people such as Paul Davies, Peter Gould and Paul Rowley began their careers on the BBC and ITV news, and Nick Pollard later became head of Sky News. Rob Jones, of course, had moved to pastures new with Radio Luxembourg, and Chris Jones and Paul Jordan would both work on BBC Radio 1 for a time.

Then in 1984 a Government White Paper came in which was designed to create choice. It was deemed unfair that one station should broadcast from two bands, so they would now have to come up with something different for each one. Stations were given a period of seven years in which to do this.

On 23rd October 1989 Radio City officially split, becoming City FM on 96.7 fm, and City Talk on 1548 am. City FM would continue to be a music driven station retaining popular DJs such as Tony Snell, while City Talk aimed to continue the old 194 Radio City's popular format with extended news coverage, phone-ins etc. Johnny Kennedy would end up here. City Talk would only broadcast between 7 am and 7 pm, however City FM continued to run 24 hours a day.

But things had been changing gradually for City in the two year period up until then. Selector Software had arrived from America and would choose a

194 Radio City

playlist based on the most popular music that would be played throughout the day. Speaking for myself, I feel this was the beginning of the end for good radio, however DJ Paul Jordan, who was there at Radio City during the change, remains adamant that this was a good thing. "Radio stations are less personality based now and have to stick to a particular type of music, depending on the station, so for example now City has a listener band between the ages of 15 and 45 or thereabouts." And woe betide anyone who plays anything which doesn't fit into that format or tries to be spontaneous or a little bit different. Big Brother is watching you and your job could be on the line. Is this really what we as listeners want? The big companies now believe they know exactly what we like and will provide it. It is all analysed by the people who run the corporations, and this, unfortunately, has progressed to the record companies, so potential musicians have to have a hit record immediately, otherwise they are dropped from their label. It really is no coincidence that much of what we hear today musically is depressingly bland.

However I don't like being told what to listen to by City or any radio station. I should be able to hear a vast array of music of all genres, not the narrow one each station has now, forcing me to constantly retune - and that 'choice' between channels is hardly accurate. So many of them play the same sounds at the same hours every day, and because of the move away from personality based DJs to ones who conform to a standard format, it all seems so bland. Very few presenters truly stand out these days. Perhaps it was no coincidence then that this all began to happen around the time that I dropped Radio City altogether, choosing instead to listen to John Peel on Radio 1 - one person who was able to continue to do his own thing - or by simply finding my own stuff thanks to reviews in the music press and attending live gigs. On the whole, radio as a vital medium became much less important to me. It would be quite a few years before I began to listen again to the odd programme on Radio City, and I would never again embrace a radio station so completely as I had the old 194.

But there is some hope emerging, and it comes from America. Chris Jones, who remembers those golden years with their flexible approach to music has this to say about then and now. "In those early days we took a pile of discs, vinyl then, into the studio and played them to match the mood. It worked then, and guess what? Management of stations in the US now think think that should be the norm. It should be like your shuffle on your iPod - you never know what's coming up next." I for one agree with them. Will we see an old type City station once more, and maybe sooner than we thought? Let's conspire to consign the restricted playlist to the bin, and

The Heart of Liverpool

stop basing stations around age groups and life styles. Speaking as someone with a most eclectic taste it remains infuriating. Let the theme begin and end with a particular programme, but can we please once again have a station that everyone can listen to every day? Something with variety that is home-grown and has its own very individual style. The manifesto that was first handed in by Terry Smith over 30 years ago still rings true today. Maybe it won't be too long before we see a change again.

Where are they now?

Roger Blyth – died 1997

Carolyn Brown - Presenter on BBC Radio 4 (www.bbc.co.uk/radio4/presenters/carolyn-brown.shtml)

Bob Buckle – musician (www.bobbuckle.com)

Billy Butler – BBC Radio Merseyside (www.bbc.co.uk/england/radiomerseyside)

Joe Butler – Most recently Saga Radio, West Midlands.

Brian Cullen – Radio Maldwyn (Magic 756) covering mid-Wales

Paul Davies – ITV News (www.itn.co.uk)

Ron Davies – died 2003

Graham Dene – Magic FM, London (www.magic.fm)

Phil Easton – Magic 1548, Liverpool

Dave Eastwood – died 1989

Michael Green – Senior lecturer in journalism at The University of Central Lancashire

Howard Hughes – Recently worked as a presenter on Talk Sport (www.theunexplained.tv) now on Smooth FM, London

Johnny Jason – BBC World Service News

Paul Jordan – Managing Director at Rock FM and Magic 999 (www.magic999.com/PaulJordan)

Chris Jones – Presenter at BBC Radio Lincolnshire (www.bbc.co.uk/lincolnshire)

The Heart of Liverpool

Mark Jones – Magic 1548, Liverpool, and corporate PA hire (www.altitudeproductions.com)

Rob Jones – Head of USP (www.usp-group.com)

Kevin Keatings – Now works for Sky Sports (www.sysports.com)

Johnny Kennedy – Presenter on Dune FM (www.dunefm.co.uk)

Paul Leckie – Manager of a Civil Service Communication Centre, Liverpool

Peter Levy – Presenter on BBC Look North (Lincolnshire and Yorkshire). (http://www.bbc.co.uk/england/looknorthhull/)

Dave Lincoln – 100.4 Smooth FM (www.smoothfm.com)

David Maker – Still working in Radio. In 2005 he previewed a potential new radio station in Liverpool, Liver FM, whose staff included, amongst others, Paul Leckie, Bill Bingham and Roy Saatchi

Arthur Murphy – Continues to work in Ireland in both TV and radio and as a newspaper columnist

Gillian Reynolds MBE – Nationally renowned Radio Critic and broadcaster. She was awarded her MBE for services to radio

Paul Rowley – BBC News Presenter (bbc.co.uk)

Terry Smith – Head of Radio City and Magic (www.radiocity.co.uk)

Tony Snell – BBC Radio Merseyside (as above)

Roy Saatchi – Head of Saatchi Associates, media consultancy

Norman Thomas – BBC Radio Merseyside (www.bbc.co.uk/england/radiomerseyside)

Clive Tyldesley – ITV Sport (www.itv-football.co.uk)